K. B. HAUGHT

DISCERNING IDOLS

HAVING A *God* EMPOWERED® HEART

God EMPOWERED®

Discerning Idols

Library of Congress Cataloging-in-Publication Data
Haught, Karen, 1957 –
Discerning idols / Karen Haught.
p. cm.

1. RELIGION / Christian Life / Personal Growth 2. RELIGION / Christian Life / Spiritual Growth 3. RELIGION / Christian Ministry / Counseling & Recovery

Printed in the United States of America by Intendion. Cypress, TX

Printed edition: ISBN-13: 978-1-938533-00-6
ISBN-10: 1938533003
Digital edition: ISBN-13: 978-1-938533-01-3

Library of Congress Control Number: 2016920084

kbhaught@godempowered.com www.godempowered.com

Dedication

To Jim, my husband of twenty years: May God continue to bless our marriage, molding us more and more into the image of His Son.

To Stephen, Keri, Paige, and Aubry: May you and your families, for generations to come, know God and the peace that comes from Him through Christ.

I have been crucified with Christ. It is no longer I who live, but Christ who lives in me. And the life I now live in the flesh I live by faith in the Son of God, who loved me and gave himself for me (Galatians 2:20).

Books by K. B. Haught

The God Empowered® Wife: How Strong Women Can Help Their Husbands Become Godly Leaders (2008)
(Available in Spanish as "La Esposa Fortalecida Por Dios." Coming in Portuguese, Swahili, Arabic, and Chinese)

Discerning Idols: Having a God Empowered® Heart (2017)
(coming in Spanish)
Discerning Idols Lite (2018)

Maura: A God Empowered® Case Study (2018)

Karen Haught
kbhaught@godempowered.com
www.godempowered.com

How to Use This Book

This book was designed primarily for counseling training, however it is as suitable for individual study or group study, or studying with a counselee. As a group study, I recommend at least one twelve-week or two six-week periods, as indicated below.

I find many people enjoy repeating the study, as each class series is unique, depending on the individuals participating and the life challenges they are facing at the time. The only additional material needed is your Bible: everything else is included. As a leader, read through the book and apply it to your life first, so you can encourage the group by sharing your testimony of how God is moving in your life regarding idolatry.

On a limited time frame, schedule one 12+ week or two 6+ week sessions to cover the material. Any additional weeks should be applied first to Chapter 6, then to Chapters 13, 10, and 9 in that order. Each week, cover key points, answer questions and share testimonies. If time allows, read some of the dialogues out loud.

Week 1 – Chapter 1
Week 2 – Chapters 2 & 3
Week 3 – Chapter 4
Week 4 – Chapter 5
Week 5 – Chapter 6
Week 6 – Finish 6, Cover 7
Week 7 – Chapter 8
Week 8 – Chapter 9
Week 9 – Chapter 10
Week 10 – Chapter 11
Week 11 – Chapter 12
Week 12 – Chapter 13

Note:

I use the phrase "please God" to describe the desire to honor God in thought, word, and deed. While it is easy to focus only on "word" or "deed," all words and deeds begin with the thoughts and intents of the heart. Keep in mind, while reading, that the primary concern is always with the heart. Obedience and good deeds carried out with an insincere or self-focused heart do not honor God.

Table of Contents

An 8.5" x 11" laminate version of the Idols Chart, with the Idols Test questions and reference notes for chapters 1-5, is available on my website www.godempowered.com.

Discerning Idols

Foreword

This book was written to help laypersons, ministerial staff, and counselors apply biblical truth to the messy and often painful situations in their own lives and the lives of others. It includes dozens of real-life examples demonstrating first-hand how idolatry destroys, and how faithfully God blesses those who relinquish their idols and surrender themselves to Christ.

While these examples provide hope and encouragement, it is important to note they are simply accounts of what actually happened, not necessarily scripts to follow. God works uniquely in every hurting person's life. On the other hand, God's Word is true. Therefore, the general prescription of worshipping God alone and seeking to please Him is always applicable, regardless of the circumstances.

Nothing written here should be construed as psychological or professional counseling, legal advice, medical advice—or advising against those things. *An individual should always seek the advice of their medical provider for medical or pharmaceutical issues and questions.*

Every example and story has been shared with permission, and conversations have been presented word-for-word as much as possible—although of necessity many have been condensed. The emails and testimonies are in the individuals' own words, so that readers might see for themselves how God changes hearts. Since my ministry is to women, most of the stories are from a woman's perspective; but the truths presented are the same for men.

Some people believe the term "idols of the heart" is unbiblical. I respectfully disagree. Ezekiel chastises God's people for taking their idols into their hearts, and the New Testament frequently associates serving desires as a form of idolatry.

Essentially, idolatry is just an expression of worship or trust for the future in something other than God. Physical idolatry is the worship of an object believed to have the power to satisfy our desires. Heart idolatry is the worship-behind-the-worship: the trust placed in our desires as requirements for our happiness and peace.

If you are using the principles in this book to help someone else, don't dwell on the past or try to "analyze" that person's heart. Jesus did not do so. He met hurting people where they were, spoke the truth in love, and pointed them to God. You can do the same by walking with others as they submit their heart to the Holy Spirit, and by rejoicing as God reveals what He would have them know.

Guard against the temptation to make an idol out of a desire to "have no idols" or "fix" someone else. Instead, let a growing understanding of idolatry lead you to greater awareness of your tendency to sin and inability to overcome that sin by your own will, strength, or wisdom. Then, set your heart on Christ—for in Him alone are joy, peace, and life found.

- Karen

Section 1

Discerning Idols

What causes quarrels and what causes fights among you? Is it not this, that your passions are at war within you? . . . You ask and do not receive, because you ask wrongly, to spend it on your own passions (James 4:1, 3).

1. The Choice

In every circumstance of life—really, in every *moment* of life—a person has a choice to seek to please themselves or seek to please God. These aren't exact descriptions, because no one ever really pleases himself or herself, except in the most temporary sense of the word (Proverbs 27:20); and "God is not served by human hands as though He needed anything" (Acts 17:25). In fact, it's impossible to please God apart from faith (Hebrews 11:6).

"Pleasing Self" and "Pleasing God" are just simple ways to describe the competing desires of the human heart to worship, trust, love, and serve its own desires—or worship, trust, love, and obey God. Since it is impossible to serve two masters at the same time (Matthew 6:24), the Y-chart below depicts these as mutually exclusive desires.[1]

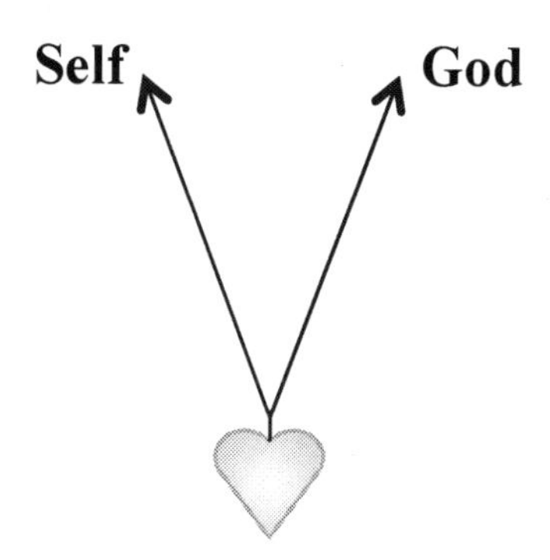

You might think trying to please another person should be a third option, but it's really just a secondary one of either of the other two. If you give someone a gift, for example, you might not expect one in return; but you probably hope to make that person happy and will watch their response to see if you were successful. If they're happy, you're happy. If they reject your gift, you're disappointed, even angry. Your vested interest in their response is evidence of an underlying motivation to please yourself—even if just for the satisfaction of knowing you made someone else happy.

Atheists are fond of saying: "Everything everyone does is for selfish reasons,"[2] and that's a true statement, from *their* perspective. A person can hardly desire to be pleasing to God if they don't believe He exists. For those of us who *do* believe in God, however, seeking to please Him is at the core of our faith. It is the very *evidence* of our faith.

> *Whoever has my commandments and keeps them, he it is who loves me (John 14:15).*

> *Faith by itself, if it does not have works, is dead (James 2:17).*

When your motivation is to please God, your eyes are fixed on Him and your joy is made complete by doing what you believe is pleasing in His sight. You might still notice the other person's response, but the nature of it will not affect your joy. If they reject your gift, you won't be upset or worry about having made a mistake. You will simply continue seeking to please God, trusting Him to use your efforts for His purposes and glory.

1. The Choice

☙ ❧

We were all born on the Self-pleasing side of the chart, and that is all we know before we put our trust in Jesus. Even *after* becoming believers, we swing back and forth from one side to the other—desiring to please God one moment and desiring to please ourselves the next. Sometimes, it seems we live in two different silos: one where we worship God, read the Bible, and enjoy His supernatural peace; and another where we deal with all the messy, practical realities of everyday life.

It doesn't have to be that way. God's intention for us is to have a *living* faith, so entwined with our daily lives that the desire to please Him never leaves our thoughts. We might not always succeed; but we can join Paul in saying, "Whether we are at home or away, we make it our aim to please God" (2 Corinthians 5:9).

☙ ❧

The effort of trying to please ourselves is a never-ending one. "If only _____________, then I'd be happy," we tell God again and again. However, once the celebratory dust of success has settled, the same restless discontent as before creeps in. We actually *feel* happier when we are pursuing a goal with a reasonable chance of attaining, than after we have attained it.

Conversely, we don't have to utterly fail at achieving a desired goal in order to feel completely miserable. When our motivation is to please ourselves, the tiniest stall in forward progress is enough to cause despair, and a goal just out of reach is more tormenting than one that is impossible to attain.

Suppose, for example, a woman finds a particular man attractive and desires a date with him. If a first date is offered, she is very happy. Should the evening go well, her desire and focus will shift to having a second date, then more. At some point, however, additional dates will stop making her happy, because the dates themselves were never the source of that happiness. If they were, a thousand dates would make her a thousand times happier than the first, but they don't.

In fact, once her heart shifts again—to desiring a commitment, for example—additional dates will begin making her *unhappy,* as a constant reminder that a commitment is not forthcoming. Should a commitment be gained, her heart will shift to new desires, such as planning the perfect wedding, finding the right house, having children, etc. (These truths would naturally apply to her husband, as well.)

> *How weak and spent with longing and lust is your heart and mind, says the Lord God (Ezekiel 16:30 AMP).*

The underlying theological truth is that what we really crave is not the satisfaction of any *particular* desire, but the power to satisfy our desires—whatever they may be and whenever they may arise. The moment we clutch any desire as though our happiness depended upon attaining it, we slip from worshipping God to worshipping His blessings. Then, our prayers no longer consist of asking God how we can please Him, but of telling God how He can please us.

In the end, as King Solomon said, it is all vanity and a striving after the wind (Ecclesiastes 1:14). The only thing that will ever truly satisfy the longings of the human heart is a relationship with God, through Christ.

ᏨᏇ

Any time we are seeking to please ourselves, we have put our trust for the future in what we desire, rather than in God. This leads us to the habit of **Controlling for Success** as evidenced by these five steps:

Desire — Plan — Act — Watch — Judge

1. First, we decide what we **desire**. That sounds simple enough—except for the fact that our hearts are full of conflicting desires. "I just want ___________!" we might say, but there are many layers to that desire, and other desires that complicate or compete with it. So, we must decide which one we think is currently most important for our future happiness. (This includes desires that are deliberately chosen, as well as those that seem to arise unbidden in our mind or heart.)

2. Second, we decide on a **plan** for trying to bring about what we desire, by mentally rehearsing different scenarios or conversations and possible outcomes. Ironically, the less certain we are which plan would be best, the more firmly fixated we become on the one we finally choose.

3. Third, we **act** by initiating that plan, anxiously following it to the letter. Should anyone or anything hinder it,

we will experience considerable discomfort, agitation, or anger—and a very strong urge to remove or eliminate that hindrance.

4. Fourth, we **watch** closely to see the results.

5. Finally, we **judge** those results. If they meet our expectations, we celebrate and start over with a new desire. If not, we modify our plan and try again, or retry the same plan with greater determination. Should repeated attempts fail, we then shift focus from trying to get what we desire to "proving" we never wanted that desire in the first place—or at least no longer do. Then we blame it all on someone else.

ᏣᏕ ᏍᏆ

Unlike the desire to please ourselves, the desire to please God has only two steps. These, I call **Obedient Faith**:

Desire — Act

There is no need to weigh all of our desires or decide which one we want or need the most, because the desire to please God supersedes all the others. There's no need to figure out a plan for how to please God, because He says how to please Him in His commands. There's no need to watch for the results or judge whether they are sufficient, because we know the results are up to God to measure. Our contentment rests in Christ's love for us and our love for Him.

That doesn't mean we are to be idle. We are to *diligently* exercise the faith given to us—supplementing it with virtue, knowledge, self-control, steadfastness, godliness, affection, and Christian love, so that we will *not be idle* or unfruitful unto the knowledge of our Lord Jesus Christ (from 2 Peter 1:5-8 AMP).

In other words, we can still have goals or desires; we just can't make our happiness dependent on achieving them. If we do, we set ourselves against God in two ways: first, by presuming we know what is best for the future; and second, by putting our trust and happiness for the future in those desires, rather than Him.

> *Many are the plans in the mind of a man, but it is the purpose of the Lord that will stand (Proverbs 19:21).*

ଓ ଛ

It is possible to think we are trying to please God, while still trying to please ourselves. Doing good works to earn our way into heaven could be one example. "Naming and claiming" God's promises or reciting specific scripture in hopes of gaining a particular blessing could be another. Even things like building a ministry or starting a new church can be self-serving pursuits if our happiness depends on succeeding. The idea that a passionate pursuit of godly perfection could be self-serving can be difficult to understand, but any time we are trying to "figure out God" in order to get what we want, we are worshipping our own desires, not God—no matter how godly our behavior might seem.

ଓ ଛ

We can always check the underlying motivation of our heart, by asking ourselves this question:

Does my happiness depend on getting a certain result?

Or in reverse:

If I were certain pleasing God would lead to what I fear, or hinder what I desire, would I still seek to please Him?

If the answer to the first question is, "Yes," or to the second, "No," then our motivation is self-serving. A heart set on what we hope to gain by pleasing God is a heart that isn't really seeking to please God at all.

☙ ❧

"I tried dealing with a situation regarding my son last week, with a pure heart," Janet said angrily. "It didn't work."

"What didn't work?" I asked, knowing her words pointed to a self-serving motive.

"You know, trying to please God. Not telling my son it had to be my way or the highway. I was very kind and calm."

"What happened?"

"Well, he has been living with us since his divorce, and generally it's been fine. The biggest problem is that he is incredibly messy. It makes me angry, because I can't stand the mess. He knows how much it bothers me, but he does it anyway, and I end up having to clean it up myself or nag and complain until he gets around to it. This time, I just calmly pointed out how much it bothers me and explained the benefits of being neater. I even offered to help, but we still ended up in a horrible argument."

"It sounds like you confused having a sincere heart with having a pure one," I said. You *sincerely* wanted your son to change and were trying to please God in how you addressed that, but you were still trying to bring about what you wanted to see happen."

"I don't get it," she said. "It's our house and we're letting him live there. Don't we have a right to expect him to honor that? What's wrong with asking him to change?"

"I'm talking about your heart, not about your decisions or words. You probably said something like: *'I would appreciate it if you wouldn't make such a mess. If you cleaned up after yourself, things would stay orderly and then you could find things more easily and not waste time.'"*

"Something like that," Janet said, nodding.

"There's nothing wrong with that. Except that in your heart, you were probably thinking: *"'I am SO frustrated! I hate it when you make such a mess. This is our house, and we are allowing you to live here. The least you could do is respect our wishes. I can't even say anything, without you getting angry at me. I am not your servant. You are an adult and need to act like one. No wonder your wife divorced you.'"*

"Yes," she replied. "How did you know?"

"Because it's what we all do. I don't know if you were more concerned about your son's messiness, his disregard for your wishes, your desire for him to care enough to do the right thing, or maybe that you somehow failed in parenting him—but if *anything* other than pleasing God was the goal of your effort, you were trying to please yourself."

"So, I'm supposed to just let him do whatever he wants in our house?" she asked, incredulously.

"No. Once you set your heart on pleasing God alone, you can still address the situation. It's not necessarily more godly to say nothing or to speak up, let him continue living there or make him leave—and a biblical argument could be made for any of those things. The important thing is that your motivation be to please God, no matter what you choose to do."

☙ ❧

Asking God to reveal His will for a decision we need to make can also be self-serving, if our request is motivated by a desire to know the future in advance or protect our future happiness. Being willing to go with either option doesn't mean our heart is purely fixed on God. It might just mean the balance of risk-to-reward is unclear or similar for both.

Theologically speaking, we can't be outside of God's will, because He works everything according to the counsel of His will (Ephesians 1:11) and always accomplishes it (Isaiah 46:10). So, the question isn't really one of being in or out of God's will, but of being blessed or devastated as His will is expressed.

As long as none of the options we are considering is in violation of God's commands, *which* road we choose to walk is far less important than *why* and *how* we walk the road we choose. God is sovereign and the future is in His hands. He works *everything*—even mistakes and missteps—for the good of those who love Him and are called according to His purpose (Romans 8:28).

> *Commit to the Lord whatever you do, and He will establish your plans (Proverbs 16:3).*

CB ED

When our pastor left his position at a relatively large church to accept leadership of our congregation, the relocation meant his children had to leave their small, Christian school. Several people expressed concern about them attending public school; but for various reasons, neither homeschooling nor private school were viable options.

Rather than become dismayed about sending their children to public school, the pastor and his wife focused on the *manner* in which they sent their children to school. Each morning, they gathered the family before breakfast for a short Bible reading, devotional, and prayer. He volunteered in the mentoring and sports programs at the school. She offered friendship and care to other mothers at the school. The entire family fellowshipped with families of their children's classmates, bringing the light and love of Christ to people who were not otherwise familiar with it.

There have been some challenges along the way, but God has turned each of them into blessing as the family has continued to seek to please God. The children are thriving academically and learning to examine, defend, and express their faith among non-believing friends in ways they never had to do with like-minded peers. Some of their friends' families have started attending church. Others have joined the wife's Bible study or asked to know more about Christ.

The point isn't that one type of schooling is better than another, but that the desire to please God in all circumstances matters more than the circumstances. Even homeschooling or private schooling could be pursued in a manner displeasing to God, if undertaken with a heart full of idolatrous fear of the world. God works in all situations to glorify His name and bless those whose hearts are set on Him.

ଓ ଡ

A third example of seeking to please God for self-serving reasons could be asking Him to reveal His purpose for our life, when the desire to know comes from a restlessness to *do something* and self-assured confidence in our readiness to begin. If He were to reply that His purpose was for us to keep doing exactly what we are already doing, in a more God-pleasing way than before, would we be disappointed? If so, then it is our own glory we are seeking, not His.

Living as we do in a society that glorifies the pursuit of "big, audacious"[3] goals and the people who accomplish them, it seems wrong—ungodly, somehow—to *not* have a significant desire or goal. Even in the church, we tend to treat big or noteworthy activities undertaken in the name of God as more impressive acts of faith than, say, loving a spouse, raising children to love the Lord, or sharing the Gospel with a neighbor. However, the desire to please God can't be divided into significant or insignificant activities or tasks. We are to seek to please Him at all times, in all things.

> *Whatever you do, work heartily, as for the Lord and not for men, knowing that from the Lord you will receive the inheritance as your reward. You are serving the Lord Christ (Colossians 3:23-24).*

☙ ❧

Over a decade ago, I was walking along the edge of a pond in our neighborhood, thinking how much I longed to do something meaningful in the world for God. That certainly seemed like a good and godly goal. Tossing a rock into the water, I watched as the ripples raced across the surface of the pond in every direction and thought, *"I want my life to be like that rock, God. I want to serve You and impact the world for You. What is Your purpose for me? What do you want me to do?"* The reply I felt the Holy Spirit whisper in my heart was this:

> *What if God's purpose for you is to be like a pebble so small that when it is dropped into a pond, that it slips silently and unnoticed to the bottom, without making even a tiny ripple?*

Normally, the idea my life might have so little apparent significance would have made me extremely dissatisfied and unhappy. In that moment, however, I had peace. "I accept that," I said aloud.

Then go home and stop trying to figure out how to serve God 'out there.' Serve Him where you are. Love your husband, honor your parents, care for your neighbors, tend to the things and people He has put in your life, in a way that is pleasing to Him—content that it may be all He has purposed for you.

I returned home with a completely different frame of mind and heart. Instead of preoccupying myself with trying to figure out what I could do for God, I began preoccupying myself with trying to please Him more in what He had already given me to do. These weren't distractions from "better" things I could be doing for Him, I realized. They *were* the better things, when I did them as unto the Lord; and in the end, it was through *those very things* God gave me opportunities to serve Him best, in places and ways I could never have imagined.

☙ ❧

Only rarely has God ever revealed His plan for an individual's life, and it's not likely He would do so for us. He probably knows we would either protest we weren't qualified—as Moses did when God told him to lead His people out of Egypt (Exodus 4:10)—or try to bring about that purpose by our own strength, as Sarah did when she gave Abraham her slave to produce the heir God had promised (Genesis 16-17).

Furthermore, He tends to bring about His plans and purposes in ways quite contrary to human expectations or strength, and often through hardship that tests and refines our faith. So, rather than asking God to tell us His purpose for our lives, perhaps we should be asking Him to *prepare* us for those purposes—whatever they might be. Then, perhaps we should look at the most difficult area of our lives as the place where He has already begun.

ଔ ଓଔ ଓ

Chapter 1 ~ Homework

1. Describe a recent situation in which you were trying to control for a particular outcome (Control for Success):

2. Describe a recent situation in which you were seeking to please and obey God, without regard for reward:

3. Describe a recent situation in which you thought you were trying to please God, but realize now you were really seeking to please yourself:

4. Write the two "heart check" questions you can ask yourself to check your motivation (See p. 12):

Chapter 1 - Prayer

Oh Lord,

Give me wisdom and discernment to know when my heart is seeking to serve its own desires, that I may diligently and continually turn my heart back to You. Where I am not pleasing You, convict me to repentance, so that I might have the contentment of putting my trust in You. Where my heart is clinging to its own ways, reveal it. Fill me with awe of Who You are, grant me the wisdom that comes by Your Holy Spirit, and soothe my heart with the joy and peace that come from Christ alone (from Romans 15:13). Give me godliness with contentment, which is the greatest gain (1 Timothy 6:6). In the name of Jesus Christ, who set me free, amen.

Journal

In your journal, list every year since you were born in a single column down the middle of however many pages as necessary. Add every key event (good or bad) in your life that you can remember on the right side of that list, next to the appropriate year(s).

2. The Desire to Please Self

The saying "God loves me and wants me to be happy" sounds reasonable enough. God does love us. We do want to be happy. So, surely He wants us to be happy, too. Unfortunately, this conclusion rests on the underlying presumption that we are basically good, and that what we desire is therefore good as well. The godliness of our desires is rarely, if ever, questioned.

It is true that a life lived in God brings great joy. However, if we believe God's highest expression of His love is to merely make us happy, then when we're happy we will have little further need for God. When we are unhappy, we will either doubt His love, or we will look for something or someone else to change. Then, we will justify that change—no matter how ungodly or destructive it might be—by saying we are sure God wants us to be happy.

To those of us raised in the United States—where the pursuit of happiness and a belief in God are deeply entwined, this seems perfectly natural, even obvious. However, to someone raised in a culture where being Christian means certain discrimination and persecution, imprisonment, or death, it doesn't even make sense. The disciples would certainly have recognized it as contrary to their experience:

Indeed, all who desire to live a godly life in Christ Jesus will be persecuted (2 Timothy 3:12).

Yet, over a hundred million books have been sold in the past century promoting the pursuit of happiness—and that's just counting the ones that reference God. Many have become bestsellers and some have even been used for church group studies. You probably have some on your own bookshelves. Although not always easy to identify at first, they are easy to identify by four distinct and easily recognizable characteristics:

1. An emphasis on success in achieving your desires,
2. An unspoken assumption that your desires are good,
3. Desiring "big" as a measure of faith,
4. Failure to mention sin and the need for a Savior.

It's not hard to find examples of "happiness theology." Just this morning, for example, I heard the following excerpt broadcast from one of the largest churches in America:

You just have to have faith the size of a mustard seed and know that God will move on your behalf. You can have hope. You can be happy. You can have your financial needs met. You can achieve your goals and dreams! God wants all these things for you! Paul had that kind of faith. He suffered, but he had faith and he achieved his goals: he wrote most of the New Testament! Have faith and trust that God wants your happiness. He has already put things into place for you. Now, you just need to believe, so you can experience it![4]

It was shocking to hear Paul given as a model of a self-serving heart. Read what Paul said in his own words:

> *Whatever gain I had, I counted as loss for the sake of Christ. Indeed, I count everything as loss because of the surpassing worth of knowing Christ Jesus my Lord. For His sake I have suffered the loss of all things and count them as rubbish, in order that I may gain Christ (Philippians 3:7-8a).*

Paul even called those who hunger for the things of this world "enemies of the cross of Christ":

> *I have often told you before and now say again even with tears, many live as enemies of the cross of Christ. Their destiny is destruction, their god is their stomach, and their glory is in their shame. Their mind is on earthly things (Philippians 3:18-19).*

When Paul said, "I can do all things through Christ," he wasn't giving us a formula for clinging to our own desires. He was describing the sustaining power and peace of Christ for all circumstances.

> *In any and every circumstance, I have learned the secret of facing plenty and hunger, abundance and need. I can do all things through him who strengthens me (Philippians 4:12-13).*

ʛ ʚ

The phrase, "God is love," has also become very popular and frequently quoted, so you might be surprised to know it is found in the Bible only twice—both in the very short chapter of 1 John 4. Even there, His love does not stand alone, but is intimately and inseparably connected to His provision of a Savior.

> *Anyone who does not love does not know God, because God is love. In this the love of God was made manifest among us, that God sent His only Son into the world, so that we might live through Him (1 John 4:8-9).*

In fact, every time "God" and "love" are found together in the Bible, it is in reference to one of four things—*all* of which clearly connect His love to His righteousness:

1. God's unique love for the Hebrews/Israelites
2. God's command for His own to love and obey Him
2. God's conditional love for those who fear Him
4. God's love as expressed in His provision of a Savior, so that all people are *able* to love Him.

It is impossible to separate God's love from His provision of a Savior. In fact, to tell of His love, without also speaking of sin and the need for salvation, is to perpetuate the false idea that human happiness is God's primary concern.

Therefore, the correct theology is not "God loves me and wants me to be happy," but *"God loves me and wants me to become holy—and to that end He has provided a Savior"* (Leviticus 19:2; 1 Peter 1:15-16, 1 John 4:10; John 3:16). With that as the foundation of our faith, when we are unhappy we will look inside our own heart and ask God what needs to change *there.* We will see every trial as an opportunity to be molded more by God into the image of Jesus Christ. No longer captivated by the pursuit of happiness, we will be satisfied with the goodness of God (Jeremiah 31:14).

☙ ❧

Delight yourself in the Lord and He will give you the desires of your heart (Psalm 37:4).

The original Hebrew word *nathan,* which is translated as "give" in the verse above, also means "to fulfill," "to satisfy," or "to put." Whenever we are delighting in the Lord—that is, when our satisfaction and joy are found in pleasing Him—He *satisfies* or *fulfills* our godly desires and *puts* new desires in our heart, perfectly matched to His purposes and glory. We experienced this when we first became a believer, and we experience it anew, every time we fully turn our heart to Him.

☙ ❧

Some years ago, I found myself becoming increasingly resentful about the things I normally did with joy for my husband. The more I thought about how much attention I paid to his needs, and how little it seemed he paid to mine, the more self-righteous and bitter I grew. Before long, a spirit of entitlement and resentment so overshadowed my joy of the Lord, even my "godly actions" were carried out in self-righteousness.

First, I tried being deliberately over-attentive, as if to prove my husband's sinfulness and justify my own, by emphasizing the difference in our "thoughtfulness." Nothing changed, of course, and I became convinced I was doomed to suffer the martyrdom of servant wifery for the rest of my life.

The prospect of trying to please God without reward soon made me bitter. "It's my husband who isn't pleasing You, God," I grumbled. Finally, I prayed—or rather, I began in complaint and ended in prayer:

> *Lord, it's not fair! I'm trying so hard, and he isn't trying at all. Don't I have a right to want my husband to care about me? If only he would do more around the house . . . no, it's not that. He works hard and I don't mind caring for the house. If only he wouldn't be so selfish . . . no, he's not really selfish. Oh Lord, if only he acted like he cared about my needs in the little things and proved it with acts of thoughtfulness.*
>
> *Yes, that's it. I want my husband to show he cares. (Sigh.) Okay God, I confess I am focusing more on pleasing myself, than on pleasing You, by making my happiness dependent on my husband showing me he cares with acts of thoughtfulness. Purify my heart and set it on worshipping and seeking to please You alone. In Jesus' name, amen.*

My bitterness disappeared, but I didn't exactly have the joy or peace of the Lord and I wasn't really thankful for what God had shown me. Rather, I felt *resigned* to the idea that pleasing God meant not having my own needs met.

That's not what God says, though. He just says to not be anxious and present our requests to Him in prayer, with praise and thanksgiving, and He will give us peace that passes all understanding (from Philippians 4:6-7). So, I closed my eyes again and prayed with a sincere desire to please God, while also confessing my need:

> *Lord, I praise You and love You. I thank You for revealing my sin and purifying my heart . . . and I'm struggling and could use some thoughtfulness. Amen.*

The tone of my voice was no different than if I had said, "Lord, I praise You and love You . . . and I'm thirsty and could sure use a glass of water." I'm sure God already knew my desires; but He said to present them to Him, so I did, without expectation or demand.

Although I had not had a chance to change anything in my behavior, my heart was completely changed. I was no longer worshipping the idea of my husband's thoughtfulness and no longer anxious about making "sacrifices" that might go unrewarded. God's peace filled my spirit, as He quieted my fears for the future and removed all my anxiety and resentment.

I was very surprised, then, when less than a minute later, my husband came into the room and did several thoughtful things he had never done before—things I had never even thought to ask him to do. I was touched by his care, but I was mostly moved by how quickly and powerfully God had responded through my husband to bless me. He so often answers prayers in unexpected and surprising ways, I have come to think of it as His signature—His way of making it perfectly clear it is He, and not ourselves, who determines our blessings.

If I hadn't known how the heart works, or how quickly it could turn an innocent desire into an enslaving idol of worship, that relatively insignificant struggle of everyday life could have grown and damaged our marriage as well as my fellowship with the Lord. Instead, it became an opportunity to learn how to worship God more fully and experience the truth of His ways in even the simplest, most practical aspects of everyday life.

☙ ❧

Spiritual warfare is worth mentioning in this chapter, because of the frequency with which Christians credit Satan for their confusion, discomfort, and trials. Some time ago, for example, I witnessed the following dialogue at the close of a monthly missions meeting:

> *"Now that we're getting more involved in missions," Daniel said, "we'd better be careful because Satan will be trying to attack us."*
>
> *"Yes," Shawn agreed. "Ever since we got back from that last trip to Africa, my business has been under attack."*
>
> *"I had a flat tire yesterday, and my daughter suddenly became ill," added Luke, "but the doctors*

can't figure out what's wrong. The devil sure gets mad when God's people are working for the Kingdom."

"I've been sick, too," said Leah, "and the plane I was on last week had to make an emergency landing because of a fire in one of the engines. It was terrifying."

"Yes, Satan is definitely trying to keep us from doing the Lord's work," Daniel said, as the others nodded.

Were we so righteous, I wondered, that Satan needed to attack us to make a mess of things? Knowing how we each struggled with sin, he might do just as well leaving us to our own devices. Besides, wasn't God sovereign—even over Satan? It seemed we were treading dangerously close to self-righteousness and denial of God's sovereignty.

In the Bible, Joseph was betrayed by his brothers, sold as a slave, framed for a crime, and imprisoned; but he never claimed Satan was trying to "take him down." He didn't "stand on the promise" of the vision God had given him, or "bind up and cast out" whatever seemed to be hindering that vision. He simply sought to please God in all circumstances and at all times (Genesis 37, 39-41). Likewise, Abraham, Ruth, Isaac, Rebekah, Jacob, Noah, Esther, Daniel, Paul, the disciples, and many others whose lives are found in the Bible also experienced suffering, but they didn't blame Satan, either.

The one man who would seem to have had a right to accuse Satan for his suffering—a man called righteous by God and whose trials were specifically attributed to Satan—was Job.

Yet Job never even mentioned Satan. He acknowledged God as the source of his trials, and the Bible says, "in all this Job did not sin or charge God with wrong" (Job 1:22; 2:10). Job sinned when he began proclaiming his own righteousness and accusing God of being unjust. He sinned in thinking he belonged to himself and had rights before God.

Paul says, "If we judged ourselves truly, we would not be judged (by God); but when we are judged by the Lord, we are disciplined, so that we may not be condemned along with the world" (1 Corinthians 11:32). Paul's request for God to remove a thorn in his flesh, which he called "a messenger of Satan," was three times refused. "My grace is sufficient," God told him, "for My power is made perfect in weakness" (2 Corinthians 12:7-10).

Knowing that God disciplines us for our own good so that we may share in His holiness (Hebrews 12:10), we should not be too quick to point to Satan in the midst of our difficulties or bind him up at every hindrance. We might just be trying to "bind up" some very important work God is trying to do in us. A better way to close our missions committee meeting, then, might have been something like this:

> *Now that we are involved in missions, we are wearing God's "logo," and surely He will be refining and disciplining us more and more. As we aim to represent Christ well, let us pray the Holy Spirit will convict us of willful sin, show us where we are in disobedience, teach us what He would have us to know, and refine our faith (John 14:26; 16:8). May God protect us from those who would cause us*

harm and glorify Himself through our lives, no matter what may come. May we be sober and alert, unmoving in faith, resisting temptation, and standing in prayer against evil, with a pure and sincere devotion to Christ (2 Corinthians 11:3). May we turn from desires that enslave us, seek to please only God by confidently trust in His authority and faithfulness.

ঞ ঌ

There is certainly a time and place for proper spiritual warfare. Jesus delivered people from demons. He also told a parable about binding up the strong man and plundering his goods (Mark 3:27). He was referring His binding up of Satan in order to "plunder" unbelievers unto Himself for salvation, however, not to delivering believers.

As believers saved by grace, we are redeemed and no longer belong to Satan (Ephesians 2:1-10), but we may wander back to Satan's "house" and voluntarily put on his iron shackles again—more comfortable with familiar slavery to sin than freedom in Christ. However, we are no longer legally bound.

> *Now that you have come to know God, or rather to be known by God, how can you turn back again to the weak and worthless elementary principles of the world, whose slaves you want to be once more? (Galatians 4:9).*

God warns that the devil "prowls around like a lion, looking for someone to devour," but He isn't talking about physical devouring. Idolatry devours us much more than any physical trial ever could, and the devil's most destructive work always begins in our hearts.

> *Beloved, if our heart does not condemn us, we have confidence before God; and whatever we ask we receive from Him, because we keep His commandments and do what pleases Him (1 John 3:21-22).*

Our spiritual warfare is to remain sober-minded and watchful, resisting the devil's temptations and standing firm in our faith (1 Peter 5:8-10), guarding our hearts, remembering our weaknesses, and being careful not to give the devil an opportunity to tempt us to sin (Ephesians 4:27). We should put on the armor of God and persevere in prayer as our plan of action (Ephesians 6:10-18). Wicked people may bring suffering or even death to our lives; but Christ has delivered us from death, and we need not fear those who can kill the body, but not the soul (Matthew 10:28).

ന്ദ ഇന്ദ ഇ

Chapter 2 ~ Homework

1. Describe "happiness theology":

2. What four characteristics do all happiness theologies have in common?

3. Note how often the pursuit of happiness played a role in your decision-making this week. Give an example.

Chapter 2 ~ Prayer

Lord God,

I know that the desires of the flesh, the desires of the eyes, and pride of life are not from You (1 John 2:16). Take away my restless longing for more than You have given me. May my only longing be for my heart to change in the ways You would have it change. I submit myself to You, desiring to please You in every aspect of my life as it is today. Replace my impatience with peace and humility. Prepare me for Your purposes and submit my will to Yours in all things, by the name of Jesus Christ, who set me free. Amen.

Journal

. To the left of the list of years of life you created in Chapter 1, write specific longings or fears you remember as being most pressing or troubling during particular times of your life, beside the appropriate year or group of years. Try to recall those that most preoccupied your thoughts or have the greatest influence on your life today.

3. The Desire to Please God

Whenever our thoughts and decisions are ruled by trying to gain what we most desire or avoid what we most fear, we are serving and honoring ourselves. Our trust for the future should rest in God, not in attaining happiness. Otherwise, we will turn God's Word upside down in an effort to get what we think we need most.

Instead of "delighting in the Lord" (Psalm 37:4), we will delight in what He can do for us. Instead of "committing whatever we do to the Lord" (Psalm 37:5), we will commit Him to what we think needs to be done. Rather than "seeking His kingdom and righteousness" (Matthew 6:33), we will seek our own kingdom of happiness. Rather than "making it our goal to please Him" (2 Corinthians 5:9), we will make it our goal to figure out how to get Him to please us.

Having a pure heart does not mean letting go of what we desire in the hope that *now* we might gain it—as in the popular saying, "If you want something badly, set it free."[5] Nor does it mean having no desires at all, which just leads to worshipping the desire of "having no desires." Our hearts were meant to worship God, and that is what God wants them to do.

Blessed is the one who trusts in the Lord, whose trust is the Lord (Jeremiah 17:7).

ශ ව

Katherine and I held tightly to our seats as our van bounced and pitched over the rough roads of Uganda. I had never paid a social visit to a witchdoctor before, so when Katherine invited me to go, I was curious.

She had attempted to visit the previous year at the request of the old woman's Christian daughter; but that visit ended poorly when the witchdoctor's son—who happened to be the most respected witchdoctor in the area—threatened to harm Katherine if she didn't leave. He had threatened his sister, too, who had moved away. Rural Africa wasn't kind to old women, and God had put it on Katherine's heart to try to visit again.

Parking beneath a small tree, we paused to wait for our translator to join us. "That's her home," Katherine said, nodding toward a rectangular mud-brick building at the back of the cleared dirt yard. "You can see her son's house in the distance, to the left. The two round huts on the right side of the yard are where she practices witchcraft. The last time I was here, the one closest to us was full of animal parts and bones hanging from the ceiling, with jars of herbs and other things lining the walls."

We walked toward the house, and wondered at a large charred area in the center of the yard. Everything was eerily quiet: even the chickens and goats that typically wandered everywhere were absent. I reminded myself that, "He who is in me is greater than he who is in the world" (1 John 4:4).

Just then, a frail-looking old woman stepped into the doorway of the house. Blinking her eyes in the sunlight, she reached up with one hand to smooth her graying hair, while brushing the dust from her faded Gomesi[6] with the other. She walked gingerly across the yard and gestured for us join her in the nearest small hut.

I went first, ducking my head under the thatch of the doorway and breathing a sigh of relief to see it was empty. The three of us, plus our translator, arranged ourselves on the hard dirt floor as best we could—the space was so small our knees nearly touched. I glanced out the doorway to see if there was any sign of the old woman's son, as I waited for Katherine to speak.

After exchanging customary greetings and polite inquiries about one another's health, Katherine asked about the charred area in the middle of the yard. To say we were surprised by the woman's reply would have been an understatement.

"All my life I worshipped the devil," she said in Swahili, our translator repeating her words to us in English. "I believed he would give me what I wanted, and I gave him everything—all my money, my chickens, my goats, everything—so he would bless me. But he gave me nothing! He is a fake and a false god!" Pointing toward the yard, she said, "That is where I burned all of my witchcraft things. Now I only worship the one true God. I have lost everything, but I am truly at peace for the first time in my life."

When we asked how she had come to know the Lord, she said a man had come a few weeks earlier and told her about the freedom she could have in Christ. That day she had accepted Jesus as her Lord and Savior.

We talked a while longer and promised to arrange for a local Christian to visit weekly to disciple her. Then we hugged good-bye with the affection of having just met a new family member. She was no longer a witchdoctor or an "old woman" to us. She was Florence, our sister in Christ.

Seven years later, Florence still loves the Lord and is active in her local church. Her son, the famous witchdoctor, has become a follower of Jesus Christ, too; and her daughter has returned with her young children to care for their mother.

ꟿ ꟿ

You and I may not be worshipping the devil as Florence once did, but we are just as guilty of worshipping other things in our pursuit of happiness—and with just as devastating consequences. The following story of a woman whose godly desire for her husband to stop looking at porn was at first an ungodly idol of her heart shows how destructive this can be.

Stephanie thought she had the perfect marriage—until she discovered her husband was enslaved to pornography. "Whenever I confront him," she said with bitterness, "he promises to stop. But within a couple of weeks he is at it again. I've agonized over why I'm not good enough for him, set aside my own desires and needs to satisfy his, trusted him every time he says he has stopped, and forgiven him every time he has slipped back into it again.

"I hate the person I've become—suspicious, worried, controlling, angry—but I don't understand how a man who calls himself a Christian can do these things. I want a husband who loves God and protects us, not one who brings evil into our home. I'm exhausted from trying so hard to please God and not seeing Him do anything. It hardly feels worth it anymore. I'm beginning to think even God can't change my husband."

It isn't wrong or ungodly for Stephanie to want her husband to stop engaging in pornography. He clearly has a sin problem, and she should pray for him and desire for him to seek the Lord. Her words reveal, however, that her underlying motivation is to please herself; for her interest in pleasing God fades when her husband doesn't change the way she wants.

Although it may not be entirely evident, Stephanie's real focus is not on pleasing God. As is always the case with idolatry, she is only able to think about how much she is hurting, how much her husband is contributing to her pain, and how hard she is trying to figure out what to do. Anger, despair, and efforts to control reveal that her happiness and peace depend on her husband changing, not on God; and it is in seeing him change that she has put her trust for the future.

That doesn't mean she should not care, or pretend his sin doesn't exist. She can still address it in whatever way seems godly and appropriate. When her heart is set on God, however, and not her own desires, those efforts will be blessed by God. It is impossible to say what will happen, but God hears the prayers of a faithful heart. He doesn't look on her husband and say, "*Wow, I don't know if I can do anything with him.*" Even if her husband doesn't change, God can still give her peace that transcends all understanding (Philippians 4:7). Something is separating her from that peace, and it isn't her husband's sin.

> *Behold, the Lord's hand is not shortened, that it cannot save, or His ear dull, that it cannot hear; but your iniquities have made a separation between you and your God, and your sins have hidden His face from you so that He does not hear (Isaiah 59:1-2).*

If Stephanie's husband were present, he would be told the same thing. Fortunately, nothing he is doing—or not doing—can prevent Stephanie from seeking to please God. Neither can his lack of participation in counseling prevent God from working and moving in the situation to His glory and her blessing. If her motivation continues to be self-serving, however, she will never have God's peace—even if He were pouring out His blessings all around her.

A right heart may result in different efforts, but she may have already been seeking to please God outwardly. What *will* definitely change is her sense of peace and the way she speaks about her situation. A person who is truly worshipping God, sounds *completely different* than one who is worshipping their own happiness. The difference will be obvious to anyone who really listens.

Instead of talking about what God needs to do in her husband's heart, she will talk about the things God is showing her in her own heart. Instead of basing her decisions on what she wants to see happen, she will base them on God's commands. Instead of complaining about her husband not changing, she will rejoice in the ways God is changing her.

☙ ❧

Helen's husband abandoned her for another woman, when their son was just six years old. He never sought a divorce and Helen believed God did not want her to take that step. She was not "standing on the promise" or proclaiming her marriage would be restored—the Bible never promises such a thing. Nor was she setting her heart on what she wanted and "waiting on God" for her husband to return. Her desire to please God stood on its own, without expectation and regardless of cost.

Soon, Helen's husband moved in with the other woman and they had a daughter. Helen's friends and loved ones stepped up their encouragement for Helen to divorce him, sharing their thoughts on scripture regarding adultery; but she believed it was most God-pleasing to stay the course.

Imagine for a moment being in Helen's shoes or advising a friend who has come to you in a similar situation. You're probably shaking your head at the thought—wondering if she was expressing trust in God, or just being naïve or legalistic in her faith. I was wondering what I would have done.

Helen continued with her story. Ten years later, he left the other woman and asked Helen to take him back. "It was the hardest thing I have ever done," she admitted, "far more difficult and painful than when he left. God had given me peace with my life the way it was, and I couldn't understand why He would allow my husband to disrupt it again. If I hadn't wanted to please God most of all, I wouldn't have been able to let him return."

I told Helen I didn't know if I could have had such faith. "How long ago did all this happen and how are things now?" I asked.

"Fifteen years," she replied, "and today, our marriage is very good."

A bit overwhelmed by it all, and trying to assess all the consequences, I asked, "What about the little girl? She lost a father, too, when he left. What happened to her and her mother?"

"Her mother is around town, but I don't see her often," Helen said. Then, she smiled and added, "But the daughter is a beautiful young woman who believes in Christ and attends our church. Even though she is not my daughter by blood, I love her every bit as much as if she were."

Awed by God's ability to turn such heartbreaking circumstances into blessing, I then remembered her son. "And your son? Surely having his father leave and suddenly return when he was a teenager must have been very difficult for him."

Helen smiled and turned toward the door where the members of the church were gathering. "Do you see the pastor?" she asked, nodding toward the man shaking everyone's hands. "That's my son."

I share that story, not to endorse legalistic teachings on marriage or divorce, nor burden those who have left adulterous marriages; but to demonstrate God's ability to bless the person whose heart is set on Him. I believe had Helen done exactly the same thing, for her own sake rather than out of a genuine desire to please and honor God, the outcome would have been very different.

> *In all your ways acknowledge God, and He will make straight your paths (Proverbs 3:6).*

CX3 80

Perhaps one of the most difficult things about seeking to please God is trying to understand *what* He wants us to do. If it's not clearly spelled out in scripture, we can ask for wisdom according to James 1:5, but it's not always easy to know whether the voice we hear in our heart is His or our own.

John and Avery's daughter, Leslie, for example, had struggled off and on with drugs since high school. When she finally got a job, they bought her a car and paid for two months' rent on an apartment to help her get on her feet. Eight weeks later, Leslie had wrecked the car, gotten laid off, and received an eviction notice from the apartment manager.

John and Avery agreed to allow her to return home on the condition she would not bring any drugs into the house, would go to church with them weekly, and would look for a new job. Less than a month later, they found her lying on her bedroom floor, unconscious from a drug overdose.

Leslie consented to go to a Christian drug treatment center; but just two weeks into the semester-long program, she called to say she was "drug-free" and wanted to come home. John and Avery knew if they refused, she would stay with friends who used drugs and probably end up on the streets, in jail, or worse. Yet, they dreaded the turmoil Leslie brought into their home and feared the negative influence she would have on their other children.

Their eldest son said it would be unforgiving to not accept her back. Their counselor said they needed to let her hit "rock bottom." Their pastor prayed with them. Their parents warned they shouldn't "enable" Leslie and should be prepared for her to steal from them if she moved back in. Friends at church said they should love her unconditionally.

John and Avery felt like they were staring into a dark unknown, desperately trying to see the future. The uncertainty of not knowing God's plan for their daughter's life, how He was going to carry out that plan, and what He wanted them to do was unbearable.

Moses probably felt much the same way when he was leading God's people out of Egypt. As the people turned back to worshipping idols, he may have thought things were falling apart. Perhaps he even wondered if he had failed God.

"If I have found favor in Your sight, Oh Lord," he said, "show me now Your ways, that I may know You and continue to find favor in Your sight" (Exodus 33:13). God assured Moses He would be with him, but Moses wanted more. "Show me Your glory," he said. But God refused to show him in advance, or while He was passing by. Only afterward would Moses be allowed to see how God's glory was revealed in and through these difficult circumstances (vv. 19-23).

We have all experienced asking God to reveal His plan for the future, in the seeming impossibility of the present. Proceeding on blind faith, with only the promise that God would go with us, was difficult. Yet afterward, as we looked back over that time period, we could we see how clearly God's glory and power had been working in our lives the whole time.

Since God's Word had no clear instruction for whether John and Avery should allow Leslie to return home, they concluded the most important thing was not *what* they decided to do, but the condition of their hearts in doing it. Relinquishing all their idolatrous desires and fears for Leslie, they no longer tried to Control for Success.

Suddenly, it was easy to resist her efforts to manipulate their affections, for her sins and weaknesses no longer filled them with fear. They had confidence God could move in her life, whether she was in their home or away.

In the end, John and Avery did allow Leslie to come home, but this time it was with faith that the future was in God's hands. When they prayed, it was no longer out of a desire to control, but out of a desire to serve God. Fear was not completely gone, but they turned that fear over to God and presented their requests with praise and thanksgiving. The peace of God, which surpasses all understanding, guarded their hearts and minds in Christ Jesus (Philippians 4:6-7) and allowed them to pray for their daughter with faith, rather than fear:

> *Dear God, we praise You and thank You for all You are doing in Leslie's life. We surrender her to You, praying that she may come to know what it means to be crucified with Christ; so that the life she lives will no longer be lived by the flesh, but by faith in the Son of God, who loved her and gave His life up for her (Galatians 2:20).*
>
> *By Your Spirit, may she no longer live according to the flesh (Romans 8:12-13), but put her trust in You, so that she might have life and have it more abundantly (John 10:10).*
>
> *Give us patience and peace as we wait, ready to do or say whatever You show us. Give us wisdom as we interact with and guide her daily. Help us fix our hearts on You, confessing our desires and fears as they arise, so they don't become idols of our hearts. May our trust be in You alone. In Jesus' name, amen.*

A month later, Leslie decided on her own to return to the treatment center, where she is currently finishing up a six-month residential program and participating in a daily Bible study. John and Avery continue to put their trust in God for the future, seeking to please Him in how they address each new situation and challenge that arises, without fear or anxiety.

ഗ ജ

As you think on these things, don't be tempted to sadly resign yourself to your fate, or say you don't care what happens. True repentance means turning from trusting in what you think is necessary and best, to trusting in God alone, without regard for what might come. That can take place only when your desire to please God is greater than your desire to please yourself.

Satan will try to whisper in your ear that God is stern and can't be trusted, that His commands are too difficult, or that you should be afraid. He will tell you that your circumstances are unique and worthy of an exception. Because of the superstitious nature of the human heart, you will fear that letting go of what you desire will cause it to *never* come to pass, or letting go of what you fear will cause it to happen. Both of those are lies: forms of New Age witchcraft that says your thoughts or emotions have the power to control your future.

Any one of us who trusts God will, at some point, be challenged to trust Him more. The conflict of wanting to hold fast to our desires while also wanting to please God is a painful one, for we fear His plans might include suffering we can hardly bear to consider.

However, there is no middle ground or compromise. Just as a spring cannot produce both fresh and salty water, we cannot worship God and our own desires or fears simultaneously (James 3:11). Only when we have truly relinquished those desires or fears and are worshipping God alone, will we find lasting peace.

> *You keep in perfect peace the one whose mind is stayed on You, because she trusts in You (from Isaiah 26:3).*

ଓ ଛଓ ଛ

Chapter 3 ~ Homework

1. Describe a recent situation in which you struggled to know how to respond.

2. What desires or fears did you have regarding that situation?

3. What would it look like to please God in that situation, without any regard for the outcome?

4. Search the word “idol” in a concordance or online Bible. (Online, do not put a space after “idol,” so it will return all versions of the word.) Write down several verses that seem most relevant to your life right now.

5. The Bible frequently contrasts the symptoms of a God-pleasing heart with a self-pleasing one in a single verse. Some examples are Proverbs 10:28, Proverbs 13:15, and Romans 8:6. Write a few favorites in the space below.

Chapter 3 - Prayer

Lord God,

I praise You and confess there are surely times I have been worshipping my own desires. I submit myself to You, oh Lord, desiring to worship You and You alone. Search me and know my heart; test me and know my anxious thoughts. See if there is any offensive way in me, and lead me in the way everlasting (Psalm 139:23-24 NIV). Where I have been in sin, Lord, use that sin for Your good and Your glory. In the name of Jesus Christ, amen.

Journal

Consider the statement, "When a heart is truly worshipping God, it cannot deliberately sin." Do you agree? Use scripture to justify your position. Describe your understanding of what it means to "truly worship God."

4. Idols of the Heart

The simplest way to describe an **idol of the heart** is "any desire in which you have such a vested emotional interest that your peace and happiness depend on it being satisfied." This always leads to pursuing that desire more than God's desires. The verse I use most often for this comes from James:

> *Desire when it has conceived gives birth to sin, and sin when it is fully grown brings forth death (James 1:15).*

By using a metaphor of human life and death, James is telling us that the spiritual law of desire, sin, and death is as sure and unbiased as the physical law of conception, birth, and death. If a child is conceived, he will be born one way or another; and once born, he will mature and grow until he dies. It doesn't matter whether he was conceived in love or violence, to a mother who was a criminal or a Bible teacher, or a father who was rich or poor. In the same way, the spiritual law of desire, sin, and death is true—no matter who we are, what we do, or how much we love God.

Notice that desire is not what is conceived, but what does the conceiving: "Desire, when *it has conceived*." When any desire—even one put in our heart by God—becomes impregnated with covetousness, it conceives *something* that leads to sin and then death. That something is an idol of the heart.

Add James 1:15 to the Y-chart, which we will now call the Idols Chart, by first writing that verse at the bottom. Then, write the word "Desire" to the left of the heart. Add the word "Sin" halfway up on the left, representing the behaviors and efforts that result from worshipping that desire. Finally, add the word "Destruction" at the top left, to represent the consequences of those efforts and clarify that the death being spoken of includes death of all kinds.

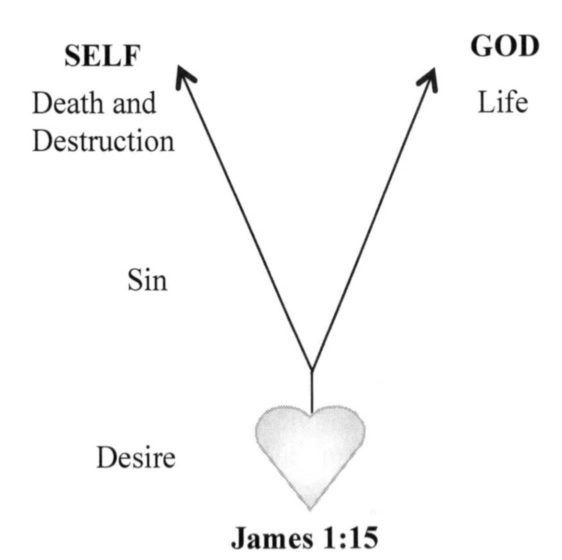

James 1:15

Desire when it has conceived gives birth to sin, and sin when it is full-grown, brings forth death.

ଓ ଓ

I frequently do a visual demonstration of James 1:15 by asking five volunteers to stand side-by-side, in what I call **The Sin Line.**[7] Using an appropriate desire for the age, gender, and purpose of the group, I ask the ***first*** person in line to point to her *mind* as she makes an observation of fact. For example, she might say, "That's a hot, fresh donut."

The ***second*** person rubs her hands together, as the factual observation becomes a desire of her *heart*. "I really want that hot, fresh donut," she says, delighting in the thought of having her desire satisfied.

The ***third*** person clinches her fists and says, "I need that hot, fresh donut!" as an indication her desire has become the focus of what might be called her physical or human *soul*—the place the Bible often speaks of as the source of a person's most passionate and intense desires or longings.

The ***fourth*** person puts her hands on her hips, stomps her foot in determination and says, "I'm going to get that hot, fresh donut, no matter what!" She is now involving her physical *strength* to satisfy that longing, quite possibly engaging in secret activities or sin to do so.

The ***fifth*** person leans over and moans, with her hands on her head in guilt and regret, representing *spirit*. If it is guilt by her own human spirit, it is false guilt—the terrible burden so often expressed in anger or hatred toward God, others, and ourselves. If it is by the Holy Spirit, then it is true guilt—the conviction of sin that leads to humility of repentance through Christ and cleansing of the conscience "from dead works to serve the living God" (Hebrews 9:14).

In a spiritual sense, The Sin Line is a downward slide, best represented by turning the Idols Chart on its side, so that seeking to please God shows as an uphill climb leading to life and peace and pleasing Self shows as a downward ramp leading to death. Once the process of idolatry has begun—though God may intervene—it is virtually impossible to stop by our own strength. Unless we have a desire to please God that is greater than the desire to please ourselves, we won't even *want* to stop.

Satan is involved, of course, but he doesn't have to do much to send us careening toward self-destruction. He just whispers the same script over and over in our ear: "*You want it. You need it. You deserve it. You have a right to it. It's not a big deal. What does God know?" (Genesis 3:4).* Like water torture, his refrain stirs up our sin nature with its rebellious desire for self-authority, until the desire to do right gives way and we dive headlong into sin—all the while justifying ourselves with his whispered words. It is so important to guard our hearts and minds in Christ Jesus, and not give the devil even a foothold.

> *Keep your heart with all vigilance, for from it flow the springs of life (Proverbs 4:23).*

> *The mind set on the flesh is death, but the mind set on the Spirit is life and peace, because the mind set on the flesh is hostile toward God; for it does not subject itself to the law of God, for it is not even able to do so (Romans 8:6-7).*

4. Idols of the Heart

☙ ❧

In some translations of the Bible, James 1:14 describes the desires of James 1:15 as evil: "Each person is tempted when they are dragged away *by their own evil desire* and enticed." We rarely think of our own desires as evil and the more strongly we hold them, the less likely we are to think of them that way: evil desires are something *other* people have.

In actuality, no desire—except that which violates the commands of God—is *inherently* evil, any more than the wood or gold of which a physical idol is made. Desires and physical things *become* evil when we worship them; because worship is an expression of trust, and our trust should be in God. Later translations—which remove the word, "evil,"—more accurately convey the applicability of these verses to *all* of our desires.

☙ ❧

The following paragraphs list common desires of the heart held in a godly and an idolatrous way, and the destructions that come from worshipping that desire:

A godly desire for *financial security* leads to tithing, saving, budgeting wisely, and working hard without neglecting other responsibilities. When that desire becomes an idol of our heart, it leads to overworking, manipulation of friends, selfishness, neglect of family, lying, cheating, bribery, or theft.

A godly desire to *care for our bodies,* stay healthy, and look our best leads us to observe good hygiene, eat nutritiously, and exercise appropriately. When that desire becomes an idol of our heart, it leads to vanity, envy, covetousness, over-exercise, overeating, preoccupation with dieting, or the overuse of plastic surgery.

A godly desire for *spiritual peace* leads us to seek to grow in holiness and godliness in every difficult situation. If that desire is an idol, we feel bitterness and resentment toward whomever we see as the source of our difficulties.

A godly desire for *someone to know how much we are hurting l*eads us to share our struggles to trust God. When that desire has become an idol, we become focused on wanting them to feel guilty or repentant, or "fix" the situation.

A godly desire for a righteous husband leads a woman to pray for her husband wisely, and joyfully serve God in honoring him. Should that desire become an idol of her heart, she will become controlling, critical, self-righteous, bitter, resentful, angry, manipulative, and covetous of other women's husbands.

Likewise, a husband with a godly desire *for his wife to honor and respect him* will pray for her and love her as God commands; but when that desire becomes an idol, he will become controlling, prideful, quick to anger, even abusive. He may use scripture to try and justify his actions.

A godly desire for *children or grandchildren to love the Lord* leads us to be a living example of faith, lovingly sharing God's Truth and striving to live in a way that is pleasing to God. If we allow that desire to become an idol, we will slip into a dogmatic approach to instruction and a legalistic approach to behavior—both of which contradict the Gospel and neglect the truth that, without Christ, we are all slaves to the power of sin.

A godly desire *to be married will* lead a single person to evaluate potential spouses wisely and observe God's commands for singleness. When that desire has become an idol of his or her heart, it may lead to jealousy, envy, fornication, self-pity, manipulation, or compromises of faith.

A godly desire *to have a child* will lead a couple to prepare themselves for the responsibilities and joys that come with parenthood. If that desire becomes an idol of their hearts, they may become preoccupied with having a child, anxious of failing, envious of new parents, doubting of God, and frustrated or angry at their inability to do what others seem to do easily.

☙ ❧

You may have noticed from those examples that the **first irony of idolatry** is that worshipping what we desire almost always leads to exactly the opposite effect. The man desperate to get married can't find a suitable spouse; or if he marries he is devastated by disappointed hopes. The woman intent on losing weight watches the scale move higher, year after year. The couple desperate to have a child fails to get pregnant, no matter how they try. The person perpetually anxious about good health and longevity struggles with one ailment after another.

Secular philosophers have observed this phenomenon, calling it "the backwards law" or "the law of reverse effort"[8]—but they don't understand why it happens. When we fix our hearts on what we think is necessary for our happiness, we set ourselves at odds with God's sovereignty. The very nature of idolatry causes us to operate in a manner contrary to His laws and consequently fail to experience His blessing.

What is true in one direction, however, is not necessarily true in reverse. Not being able to find a spouse, for example, does not prove we have an idol of wanting to be married. Not being able to lose weight does not prove we have an idol of wanting to be thin. Not being able to get pregnant does not prove we have an idol of wanting a child. Becoming sick, not being healed of a disease, or struggling with ill health does not prove we have an idol of good health. God has many reasons for the circumstances of our lives.

Even so, examining our hearts for the possibility of idolatry in all situations is wise. Although it might not have played a role in the *cause* of that particular set of circumstances, there is always the potential of it being involved in our response. If so, it will separate us from the supernatural peace and blessing of God—when and where we need it most.

Once an idol of the heart has been identified and confessed, surprising things begin to happen. First, there is God's peace. Second, there is some kind of meaningful and significant blessing. The person who relinquishes the desire to get married, may suddenly meet the "significant other" they have been looking for all along.

The parents who relinquish the longing for their child to turn his life around may suddenly see that child dramatically change for the better. The person who relinquishes an idolatrous desire to be well may be healed. The person who relinquishes an idol of losing weight may find they no longer struggle with food. The couple who relinquishes the idea of having a child and adopts, may suddenly find they are pregnant.

These things don't always happen, of course, but they happen often enough to be a commonly recognized phenomenon, even among non-believers. The spiritual law of idolatry applies to everyone, and God blesses according to His will—for *His* glory, not ours.

For a possible biblical example, we can look to Joseph who after the birth of his sons said, "God has made me forget all my hardship and all my father's house and made me fruitful in the land of my affliction" (Genesis 41:51-52). Though we have no other indication Joseph dwelt on those heartaches, the relinquishment of them implies he did. Just a few verses later, his brothers suddenly reappear in his life, and circumstances are put into motion by which he is eventually reconciled to them and reunited with his beloved father.

Our goal for relinquishing our idols should never be to get what we want. That's still idolatry. We can, however, rest in the knowledge that God will always bless the heart that is truly worshipping Him, and He knows what we most need. Even if things never change, we will have His peace; which, in a way, is a greater miracle than getting exactly what we want.

The **second irony of idolatry** is that the more we try to control for what we idolatrously desire, the less in control we feel. The world says we have only two options: cling more passionately to what we desire or throw up our hands and act like we no longer care. We do still care, of course. We're just hiding that desire deeper in our heart, the way Rachel hid her family idols and pretended they weren't there (Genesis 31:34).

God offers a third option of relinquishing what we desire by holding it with an open hand while keeping our eyes and heart on Him. That's not the same thing as "trying not to control" or resigning ourselves to our lot in life.

Those are a type of dying to Self, but not as God intended. The dying to Self God commands results in the humble praise of a joyful life—not the sighs of resignation or self-pity. If what we desire is in line with what He knows is best for us, we can trust He desires it more than we do and is far more capable of bringing it about.

The **third irony of idolatry** is that the destructive consequences we experience from worshipping an idol almost always come about by our own hands. One minute, we're willing to do *anything* to bring about what we desire. The next, we're deliberately undermining any opportunity to have it at all. We can't lose weight, so we overeat. We can't be perfect, so we self-harm. We can't get our child to obey, so we rage. We can't get our spouse to change, so we divorce. We can't have the life we desire, so we destroy the life we have.

If idolatry were just about getting what we want or attaining happiness, such self-destructive responses wouldn't make sense—even to human minds—but idolatry is really all about trying to control. Destructive behavior is just another way of trying to gain that control, when nothing else has worked.

Every way of a man is right in his own eyes, but the LORD weighs the heart (Proverbs 21:2).

☙ ❧

Madlyn couldn't remember a time when her first thought in the morning hadn't been about what she should or shouldn't eat that day, and her last thought at night hadn't been about how miserably she had failed. She weighed herself again and again—worshipping at the altar of the "holy scale"—while watching the numbers creep higher and higher.

"I know vanity is sinful, so I've been trying to be more pleasing to God by focusing on improving my health as my motivation for losing weight," she said. "I've asked God to take away my desire for unhealthy foods and give me a desire for healthy ones. But I keep wanting to eat what I know I shouldn't, and not eat what I know I should," she added, echoing Paul's thoughts on the rebellious nature of the heart (Romans 7:14-25).

If Madlyn really wants God's peace and to be led by the Holy Spirit in correct eating, she has to go deeper than simply trying to find more godly-sounding ways to worship the goal of achieving a desired weight. She has to completely relinquish her dependence on that desire as a requirement for her happiness.

☙ ❧

The minute we make our happiness dependent on some desire we hold dear, we are guilty of putting our hope for the future in the satisfaction of that desire, rather than in God. We build a temple in our heart around that desire to protect it. Then, we make sacrifices or offerings to try to bring it about, which is no different than making sacrifices or offerings to a physical idol—and just as offensive to God.

> *These [people] have taken their idols into their hearts, and set the stumbling block of their iniquity before their faces. Should I indeed let myself be consulted by them? (from Ezekiel 14:3).*

We create rules and rituals for others to honor our idols, and watch carefully to see whether they obey. If they do, they receive our blessing. If they don't, they feel our wrath. We also set rules and rituals for ourselves. When we break them—as we always eventually do—we pour out wrath upon ourselves in self-hatred, depression, and distress. Then we become angry with God.

> *When a man's folly brings his way to ruin, his heart rages against the Lord (Proverbs 19:3).*

The desire to please God must stand on its own, without concern for the result. If we have already determined what we feel is required for our happiness, peace, or fulfillment, we are already opposed to God—unless that requirement consists solely of being conformed to the image of Christ. Even painting scripture on an idolatrous desire doesn't make it godly. It just makes it an idol with scripture painted on it.

> *Who may ascend the mountain of the LORD? Who may stand in His holy place? The one who has clean hands and a pure heart, who does not trust in an idol' (Psalm 24:3-4)."*

In considering our own idolatry, we must not give into the temptation to make a new idol of the desire to "have no idols," lest we deny our need for a Savior. We cannot purify our own hearts. We can only learn to recognize when we are slipping into idolatry and quickly turn our hearts back to God.

We must also guard against the false humility of sorrowfully resigning ourselves to difficult circumstances. By the very fact of our sorrow, we belie the fact that our hearts are set more on what we think would be best, rather than on doing all we can do to the glory of God in every circumstance.

Third, we must avoid "standing on the promise" that God will bless one of our idolatrous desires, or read the Word in an effort to try to figure out how to get Him to do so. God will never bow down to our idols or bless us through them.

"I will cast your dead bodies on the dead bodies of your idols," He says, "and My soul will abhor you" (Leviticus 26:30). God will never share His glory with another god (Isaiah 42:8). He won't even bless our idolatrous desires out of compassion; for if He did, we would just worship idols more—and the end of idolatry is death.

Truly trusting God means seeking to please Him, without regard for reward or outcome. We can certainly ask God to satisfy the desires of our heart; but if our joy and peace rest in Him doing so, we have slipped from worshipping God to worshipping His blessings instead. Should it come as any surprise, then, when our prayers in those areas go unanswered?

> *"Put away the foreign gods which are in your midst, and incline your hearts to the Lord, the God of Israel." The people said to Joshua, "We will serve the Lord our God and we will obey His voice" (Joshua 24:23-24).*

ঙ ঌ

Two New Testament parables seem to instruct us to determinedly cling to our desires in a way that might be called idolatrous, in an attempt to get God to bring those desires about. We call these the "persistent parables," because our focus is on the persistent person. However, they should be called the "reluctant parables," because Jesus focuses on the *other* person in the story.

"The Parable of the Persistent Friend" (Luke 11:5-8), for example, should be called "The Parable of the Reluctant Friend" because Jesus is not teaching us to pound on God's door until He responds. He certainly is not comparing God to a man who says, "Don't bother me. The door is already locked and my children and I are in bed. I can't get up and give you anything" (v. 7). Rather, He is contrasting God—who lovingly provides for the needs of His people without delay—to a friend who only reluctantly gives what is needed after great persistence by the one in need.

> *Ask, and it will be given to you; seek, and you will find; knock, and it will be opened to you (Luke 11:9).*

Likewise, "The Parable of the Persistent Widow" (Luke 18:1-5) should be called "The Parable of the Reluctant and Unrighteous Judge" because Jesus is not teaching us to continually hound God until He gives us what we want. Neither is He comparing God to a judge who only reluctantly gives justice. Rather, He is contrasting God, whose justice is sure and certain for the people whom He loves, to an unrighteous judge who delays in giving justice—and then only out of annoyance.

> *Will not God bring about justice for His chosen ones, who cry out to Him day and night? Will He keep putting them off? I tell you, He will see that they get justice, and quickly (Luke 18:7-8).*

That doesn't mean we can't, or shouldn't, persevere in asking God to satisfy our needs; but our contentment and our trust for the future must be in Him, not in having those needs satisfied.

☙ ❧

Theologically, idolatry comes from the desire to be god of our own lives, which is the very essence of the sin nature. Created in God's image, we jealously desire to be more like Him (Genesis 3:1-6).

He gave us life: we crave His version of life in immortality. He gave us love: we long for the love due Him alone in adoration, glory, and worship. He gave us authority over the earth: we hunger for His sovereignty and control over the circumstances of our lives.

Together, these longings form the "God-shaped hole"[9] in our hearts that points us to Christ—for in Christ, we will have eternal life (John 3:16), we will be glorified (Romans 8:17, Colossians 3:4), and we will rule and reign over all the earth (2 Timothy 2:12). Any other effort to satisfy these longings, apart from Christ, is an exhaustive and destructive exercise that will never satisfy. It is sin.

No wonder tears so often accompany the decision to surrender ourselves to God through Jesus Christ. Having all of our deepest longings quieted at once, forever, is such a sweet relief.

He is our living water and in Him, we find our peace (from John 7:38).

☙ ❧☙ ❧

Chapter 4 ~ Homework

1. Draw the Idols Chart below, as much from memory as possible.

2. What are the three ironies of idolatry?

Chapter 4 - Prayer

Lord,

Show me when I am turning away to serve the desires of my heart as if they were gods (Deuteronomy 11:16) and keep my heart pure and soft, not hardened by the guilt of sin or burdened by regret. I set my eyes on You alone, Lord, longing to know Your peace and wisdom for all of life. Show me what You would have me know. Peel back the layers of my heart to reveal whatever idols might be there, so that I may repent and offer a sacrifice of praise to You—and only You—oh Lord (Hebrews 13:15). In the name of Jesus Christ, amen.

Journal

Keep a pad by your computer or bed and make a list of all the desires or fears you have throughout the week. Note which are related to those you added to your life history timeline, which reappear most often, which are most prevalent in your life right now, and which currently distract you most in your spiritual life. Choose one to explore in the following chapters.

5. The Symptoms

You might think you aren't in idolatry at this moment, and if you have the peace of God—"free of agitating passions, moral conflict, and fear"[10]—you're probably right. There will surely come a day, however, when some desire very precious to you is threatened: when anger, hurt, or fear become your constant companions; and you feel so confused and worried about you can't even think straight. All you will be able to think of is how much you are hurting, how someone else (or circumstances) is contributing to that hurt, and how hard you are trying to figure out what to do.

> *They served their idols, which became a snare to them (Psalm 106:36).*

It is not easy to identify your own idol when you are already worshipping it, because trying to figure it out just so you can ask God to take it away creates a conflict of interest that psychologists call "cognitive dissonance." However, trying to get rid of every potential idol in your heart, before you have any symptoms, is futile. It's like trying to get rid of every potential illness in your body, before you are sick.

Fortunately, there are warning signs God has put in place to let you know when your heart has strayed. "Controlling for Success" is the earliest sign—like a fever before you realize you are sick. The other two are a "downcast face" and a "tormenting spirit."

A **downcast face** includes things like despair, anger, rage, depression, bitterness, jealousy, fear, hatred, judgmentalness, or other negative feelings we have when our desires are hindered. The term, "downcast face," comes from the story of Cain, whose idolatrous desire for God's favor filled his heart with jealous anger.

God observed Cain's downcast face, urged him to do the right thing, and warned of sin to come if he didn't. Displaying the first symptoms of idolatry, Cain was at a pivotal point, and time still remained for him to repent and turn around, before being overcome by sin. Instead, he gave into sin, murdered his brother, and was cast out of God's presence and favor—his idolatry bringing about the opposite of what he most desired (Genesis 4:16).

> *Then the Lord said to Cain, "Why are you angry? Why is your **face downcast**? If you do what is right, will you not be accepted? But if you do not do what is right, sin is crouching at your door; it desires to have you, but you must rule over it" (Genesis 4:6, emphasis added).*

A **tormenting spirit,** which in some translations is called an "evil spirit from God" (AMP, NIV) or "harmful spirit from God" (ESV), is the tornado-like, blinding state of mental, emotional, and spiritual confusion of idolatry. It is essentially the absence of God's peace and wisdom.

5. The Symptoms

The idea of an evil spirit being from the Lord may seem strange. However, there are only two things that will cause someone to turn from worshipping and defending an idol: a desire to please God greater than the desire to please themselves, or pain greater than whatever they hope to gain from their idolatry. The first is given by God through the Holy Spirit. The second is given by God through a *tormenting spirit.*

The term, "tormenting spirit," comes from the story of King Saul, whose idolatrous desire for the favor of his people led God to remove the Spirit of the Lord from his life and give him an evil or tormenting spirit, instead. Saul refused to turn back to God and continued to pursue David to kill him. In the end, Saul committed assisted suicide, which resulted in David being crowned in his place—which was the very thing Saul had been so jealously trying to prevent (1 Samuel 31).

> *Now the Spirit of the Lord had left Saul, and the Lord sent a* ***tormenting spirit*** *that filled him with depression and fear. Some of Saul's servants said to him, "A* ***tormenting spirit from God*** *is troubling you"(1 Samuel 16:14-15 NLT, emphasis added).*

People often ask if that means grief, sorrow, or righteous anger are always symptoms of idolatry. Since Jesus experienced each of those emotions at various times, the answer is clearly no. However, neither sorrow nor grief makes a person righteous. Idolatry may have had no part in what caused the situation, but it may be present in the response—and often is.

ʙ ะ

A friend once asked if the story of Hannah in 1 Samuel 1 proved that God sometimes rewards idolatrous desires. Hannah certainly seemed to show all the signs and symptoms of a downcast face and a tormenting spirit, when she was crying out to God for a child:

> *She was* ***deeply distressed*** *and prayed to the Lord and* ***wept bitterly*** *. . . As she continued praying before the Lord, Eli (the priest) observed her mouth. Hannah was speaking in her heart; only her lips moved, and her voice was not heard. Therefore Eli took her to be a drunken woman. And Eli said to her, "How long will you go on being drunk? Put your wine away from you."*
>
> *But Hannah answered, "No, my lord, I am a woman* ***troubled in spirit****. I have drunk neither wine nor strong drink, but I have been pouring out my soul before the Lord. Do not regard your servant as a worthless woman, for all along I have been speaking out of my* ***great anxiety and vexation****."*
>
> *Then Eli answered, "Go in peace, and the God of Israel grant your petition that you have made to Him." Then the woman went her way and ate, and her face was no longer sad" (vv. 6-18).*

Notice when the prophet Eli said, "Go in peace and the God of Israel grant your petition that you have made of Him," Hannah's symptoms of idolatry disappeared. Confident in faith, she stopped worshipping the desire for a child and was no longer vexed or anxious. She left with a peaceful heart and countenance—surely still desiring a child, but no longer worshipping that desire.

The next morning, Hannah and her husband rose early and worshipped the Lord. Later, "Elkanah knew Hannah, his wife, and the Lord remembered her, and in due time Hannah conceived and bore a son" (v. 19). We cannot presume to know if Hannah's inability to bear a child was caused by idolatry; but there was certainly evidence of idolatry in her response—until Eli's words put her heart at ease and she rested in God alone. Her story is actually a wonderful example of God blessing the heart that is set on Him.

☙ ❧

Isabelle, a young mother and relatively new Christian, was upset because she had reason to believe her son's second grade teacher was picking on him. At first, Isabelle dismissed the situation as an exaggeration, but her concern was renewed when other parents confirmed there was a problem. Torn between speaking to the teacher and risking a backlash against her son, or letting it go and subjecting him to further criticism, Isabelle mentioned her concern to her small group.

"Should I make an appointment with the school or not?" she asked. "I am so confused."

"I don't know, but do you want to explore for idols of the heart?" Mia asked.

"Sure," Isabelle said, gratefully.

"Okay, what do you need in order to feel happy in this situation?"

"I need her to stop picking on my son."

"Why does it bother you that she picks on him?"

"Because it could hurt his self-esteem and it's not fair—he's just a little boy. Why would she pick on him?"

"Hypothetically, if she kept picking on him but you knew he would be fine, could you live with that?"

"I guess so."

"On the other hand, if you *did* get her to stop but his self-esteem was badly damaged, would you be okay with that?"

"No, I wouldn't. Just thinking about it makes me angry. I'm worried, too, that she'll find other ways to pick on him if I confront her," Isabelle said.

"So it sounds like his self-esteem is your main concern, not the unfairness of her picking on him. What about the possibility of his self-esteem being damaged bothers you?"

"I don't get the question."

"I know it sounds silly, but bear with me. I'd be upset if a teacher were picking on my child, too, but my reasons might be different than yours. I don't want to assume anything."

"I just want him to grow up happy and healthy."

"What are you afraid it might mean if he didn't?"

"That I'm not a good mother," she said, starting to cry.

"Is it possible the desire to be a good mother could be an idol of your heart?" Mia asked gently. "We all struggle with that one."

"Yes," Isabelle said, nodding.

"Do you think you are a bad mother?"

"No. I am a good mother, and I care about my son."

"It's good to care, but if you are worshipping the idea of protecting his self-esteem or being a good mom, then no matter what you do it won't go well. If you talk to the teacher, you'll feel defensive and anxious because you lack God's wisdom. If you don't talk to her, your worry will grow because you lack God's peace. Either way, your efforts won't be blessed."

"So I have to confess an idol of wanting to be a good mom and protect my son, and ask God to take it away? I don't want to not have that desire."

"You can still desire it. God probably put that desire in your heart when He gave you your child. Ask Him to take the desire to be a good mom away, as an idol; and He will purify it and give it back to you as a godly desire—with His wisdom and peace."

"Okay, but I'm not sure I trust God enough to just ignore what the teacher is doing and let it go. I know that sounds terrible, and it's not that I don't trust my son with God. I just that I feel I need to do something about it."

"No one says you can't. Just as strong a biblical argument could be made for addressing it with the teacher, as for letting it go. The important thing is to make sure your heart is not motivated by worship of anything other than God—even something as godly sounding as being a good mom."

"So, if I address it, it needs to be because I believe it pleases God—not because I want my son to be happy . . . "

"Right. God might be giving you the desire to address it for the teacher's sake, too, you know. Or to exemplify for your son how to confront and address difficult people in a godly way—which is a very valuable lesson."

" . . . and if I don't address it, it needs to be because I believe *that* pleases God—not because I'm afraid it will make things worse."

"Exactly. God might use *that* effort to demonstrate to your son how to exercise forgiveness, or how to submit to ungodly authority with a God-pleasing heart. Those, too, are valuable lessons."

"How do I know what God wants?"

"Neither option violates God's commands, so either is okay. It is the idolatry that is making you anxious and confused. Ask Him to remove it. Then whatever you choose to do, do it with a heart that is pleasing to God."

"Thanks. I think I understand now."

"This may seem off the topic," Mia added, "but you haven't mentioned your husband in all this. Why not ask his advice? Then you'll be honoring God in your marriage, even while trying to figure out what to do."

"I guess I don't bother because he usually tells me to do whatever I think is best or asks me what I want," Isabelle said.

"Well, you could try telling him the problem, without telling him what you think the solution should be and without an idol in your heart of having him respond in any particular way. Then see what God does. He's powerful enough to guide your husband, too."

"Why do I always feel like I have to figure things out on my own, first?" Isabelle asked, shaking her head and smiling.

The next week, Isabelle told Mia and the group that after praying and confessing her idolatry, she was no longer anxious about the situation, but still felt it needed to be addressed. Believing it was most God-honoring to share the problem with her husband, she was surprised when he suggested they should go together to meet with the teacher and the principal.

Instead of offering to go alone or saying it would be a waste of his time, as she might have done in the past, Isabelle decided to trust God and follow her husband's lead. During the meeting, she was amazed and appreciative for the way he spoke forthrightly with the principal—rather than wait for her to take the initiative, as he had always done before.

God gave Isabelle peace during the meeting, and not once did she feel anxious or worried about what might happen if it didn't turn out the way she hoped. In fact, she was not attached to any particular result at all, just the desire to please God in how it was addressed. As it turned out, the principal apologized for the teacher's behavior, and Isabelle and her husband accepted the offer to transfer their son to another class.

☙ ❧

One of the idols of my heart I struggled with for quite some time had to do with finishing the writing of this book—a process that took nearly eight years. The discipline to write wasn't a problem: I could type away for days on end without a care. It was the desire to finish and the idea of taking time to do anything else that made me fearful.

When I dedicated myself to writing, I worried about neglecting my husband, home, and church. When I dedicated myself to those things, I worried I might never finish writing. From time to time, I justified disobeying God in one area "for a little while," in order to try to please Him in another—and then wondered at the lack of peace in my heart. *"How can I be pleasing to You in all things, God,"* I asked, *"when there isn't enough time to be pleasing to You in all things?"*

The irony of trying not to have an idol of finishing a book on idolatry was not lost on me. In attempting to overcome that idolatry by my own strength (which was really just trying to please God without relinquishing the idol) I ended up with an idol of not having an idol of finishing a book on idolatry! As is always the case with such convoluted efforts of good works, my prayers became pleas for God to serve my own desires:

Dear God, every time I try to please You in one area of my life, it is at the expense of another. What am I supposed to do? Give me the ability and wisdom to get done all I need to do, so I can have peace again. Help me finish this chapter, help me be a loving wife, help me keep my house in order, and help me not be anxious. In Jesus' name, amen.

That doesn't sound too bad, but if you read it carefully you can see a heart focused more on my own desires and goals, than on God. When I set my mind on pleasing God, my prayers sounded more like this:

Lord, I am in awe of Your sovereign authority and grace, amazed by Your gifts of life, marriage, and family. Thank You for a mind to think and hands to write, for all You have entrusted to me, and for who You are. Cleanse my heart and remove the idols of finishing this project and trying to "be perfect." Show me how to be pleasing to You, even in my imperfection. In Jesus' name, amen.

On any given day, the sincere desire to please God might have resulted in spending more time writing, doing something with my husband or family, teaching a class, caring for our home, serving in church, or spending time with a friend. All that would have mattered was that I was "walking in a manner worthy of the Lord, fully pleasing to Him, bearing fruit in every good work, and increasing in the knowledge of God" (Colossians 1:10).

ଓ ଃ

As you read through the following true story, underline anything Chloe says that seems to indicate a downcast face or a tormenting spirit. Don't worry about trying to identify her idol or decide whether or not she is justified in her feelings. Don't try to figure out what her husband's possible idols might be. He may be sinning as well, but each person's greatest problem is the one inside his or her own heart, and no one else's sin can keep that person from seeking to please God.

Chloe poured herself a fresh cup of tea as the ladies in her small group gathered for their weekly study on idolatry. "My husband texted me on the way here, apologizing for a big fight we had last night," she said.

"Are you going to reply?" asked Layla, the group's facilitator.

"I'm not sure I want to," Chloe replied. "He can't just say he's sorry and expect me to be okay with it."

"So what happened?" Maria asked.

Chloe took a seat at one end of the couch. The other ladies sat nearby. "Yesterday morning, our oldest daughter missed the bus, and since Gavin had already left for work, I had to get the other children up and take her to school. When I got back home, the three little ones were fussy, the house was a mess, the dishwasher stopped working, and the baby threw up all over my shirt. Every time I tried to make some progress, the twins got into something and ended up fighting. I was so stressed."

The other ladies nodded in empathy.

"Gavin called at lunch," Chloe continued, "asking how my day was, but I didn't want to complain and stress him, too, so I told him everything was fine. After we hung up, though, I felt jealous. I started thinking about how he gets to go to work, talk to other adults about important things, then come home and relax. Sometimes I miss the feeling of accomplishment I used to get from working. We had agreed I would stay home with the kids—and I really wanted to—but it's a lot harder than I thought."

"I can relate," Mattie said.

"I was pretty upset, so I went on a cleaning frenzy—that's what I do when I'm upset—and I felt a lot better. Then I started thinking about how hard my husband works to support us and how blessed I am, and I felt guilty for being jealous. So, I decided to weed the front garden for him. I was in a great mood and looking forward to seeing him."

"What happened next?" Layla asked.

"He came home, walked right past the garden without noticing, changed his clothes, spent some time on the computer, and asked if dinner was ready. He didn't even comment how nice the house looked. I was so hurt. The kids had already eaten, so it was just the two of us, but we didn't talk."

Leaning back with a sigh, she continued. "He offered to do the dishes, but I told him I would do them, and he went to watch a movie on TV. At first I was angry, but I knew that wasn't God-pleasing; so after putting the kids to bed, I sat next to him. I was actually enjoying the movie—until one of the twins woke and started yelling from bed for a glass of water. I pretended not to hear, to see if my husband would respond; but he ignored it. He's their father. Why can't he do something? He didn't even take his eyes off the movie. He just turned his head a little and said, 'He's calling you.' Oh, I was so angry!"

"What did you do?" Selena asked.

"I let him have it. I said, '*You* go to work, feel valued, enjoy yourself, come home, and relax. I work all day wiping noses, cleaning house, shopping, holding crying babies; then I fix dinner, check homework, get clothes ready for the next day. When do *I* ever get a break?'"

"You just described my life," said Maria.

"I helped our son and then went to bed," Chloe continued. "Fifteen minutes later my husband came to bed. I thought we would have an opportunity to talk, but he just turned on the TV in there. I told him he was insensitive. 'My conversation consists of single syllable words repeated over and over again to three children under the age of four,' I said, 'and I need some adult conversation. You should have figured that out by now. When does everything stop being all about you?'"

"Did he listen?" Mattie asked.

"No! He got in bed, and asked if I was going to let him hold me. Can you believe that? I told him to hold his pillow! He said, 'Okay, I will. It's more affectionate than you anyway.' That hurt so much. After all I have done, I can't believe he would be so demeaning. '*You're* the one who's unaffectionate,' I told him, 'and thoughtless and self-centered! You think you have it tough, but you have no idea how hard it is for me.'"

"It sounds like it was getting out of control," Layla said.

"Honestly, it felt like our marriage was over. I didn't want him to see me cry, so I took a pillow and blanket upstairs and laid on the floor of the game room. I couldn't sleep, but he was snoring within five minutes. Obviously *he* wasn't too upset. I kept hoping he would come up to apologize and ask me back to bed, but he didn't." Sighing, she added, "It was the first time we have ever slept apart."

"Oh dear," Sharon said, concerned.

"In the morning, he came upstairs to wake the kids and tell them good-bye. When he knelt down to kiss me, I pretended to be asleep. After he left, I couldn't stop crying. I almost didn't come here today—I look awful and my heart isn't in the lesson."

A few of the ladies reached out to comfort Chloe. One said she should just forgive her husband and put it behind her. Another said she should go back to work, at least part time. A third said she should tell her husband the ways she needed him to express his love to her. Others said she had a right to be angry and needed to call a family meeting to spread out the household and parenting responsibilities more fairly. Several offered to pray for her. Each was focused on trying to help Chloe regain her happiness or change her circumstances with practical human solutions.

Layla interrupted the discussion. "Any of those ideas might be helpful; but if Chloe doesn't first consider what God might be trying to show her through this difficulty, she'll be missing the most important thing. Whatever benefit she might gain will be only temporary." Turning her attention to Chloe, she said, "You definitely testified to having a downcast face and tormenting spirit. What about feeling overwhelmed earlier in the day bothered you the most?"

Chloe thought for a moment, then said, "I used to manage very large projects at work, so I should be able to keep a home running smoothly. I really don't mind having given up my job, as long as I feel like I'm doing well in this one. Not to say that raising children and being a wife is a job, but you know what I mean."

"So, when your husband called, why were you dishonest and said everything was fine?" Layla asked.

"Whoa," Chloe said, surprised. "That sounds harsh, but I guess it *was* a lie. I thought I was just being considerate." She paused, then added, "I told him everything was fine because saying it wasn't would have been like admitting defeat."

"You could have said you were having a really rough day and feeling overwhelmed."

She frowned. "You're right. I'm not sure why I didn't."

"Even if he wasn't gracious about it," Layla said, "I don't think he would have said, 'I expect you to clean the house top to bottom, then do the weeding I didn't do last weekend.'"

"No, he wouldn't. He probably would have told me to relax, forget about the house, hire someone to clean, go do something fun with the kids, or get a sitter and take some time for myself."

"And you would have given him half a dozen reasons why you couldn't do any of those things . . .."

"Probably."

"And even resent that he suggested them?"

"Yes. I would have felt like he didn't understand or appreciate the problem."

"Which was . . .?"

"I don't know. I guess that I felt like I was failing."

"At what?"

"At everything. When I feel overwhelmed, I get angry at the kids, angry at myself, and angry at my husband."

"So, basically you're saying you pride yourself on doing a good job and feeling competent, whether at a company or as a wife and mom," Layla said. "Doing a good job could be an idol of your heart, because whenever you are succeeding at what you are doing, you feel good. Whenever you aren't, you feel angry or destructive."

"That makes sense," said Chloe.

"Suddenly deciding to clean the whole house could have been a type of offering to that idol," Layla added.

"Hmm," Chloe said, nodding. "It sounds rather obvious when you put it that way . . . and I thought I was just cleaning the house!" She smiled.

"Weeding the garden afterwards might have been a kind of 'guilt offering' for feeling angry and jealous . . . or an offering to earn your husband's affirmation and approval."

"Probably a little of both," Chloe said. "When he didn't even notice, it seemed pointless."

"What do you mean?"

"I felt like I had sacrificed all that time and effort for nothing. Oh my goodness, I just said 'sacrifice!'"

"What were you sacrificing for? What were you hoping to gain by that sacrifice?"

"I guess I just wanted his appreciation."

"Why would that have made you feel better?"

"I don't know. It probably would have made me feel like I was doing a good job. Or that I didn't have to be perfect to be loved and appreciated."

"But you were trying to be perfect to earn that."

"So, does that mean wanting to be perfect is my idol?" Chloe asked.

"It could be—or wanting to know your husband loves you, even when you feel like a failure. Which of those desires is the main one?

"I'm not sure."

"Well, would you have more peace if you felt successful in being a wife and mother, but didn't have your husband's appreciation; or if you had his appreciation, but felt like a failure?"

"When I feel successful and confident, I don't need his appreciation so much. It's nice, but I don't get upset if it isn't there. On the other hand, when I feel like a failure, no amount of his reassurance really eases my pain. It's nice to know I'm loved anyway, but I still feel anxious and confused."

"It sounds like feeling you are succeeding as a wife and mother is the idol of your heart, and trying to gain your husband's appreciation or affirmation is a way of trying to serve or satisfy that idol. If your greatest fear was not having your husband's love and affection, it might have been the other way around."

"That makes sense."

"Fast forward to when your husband came home," Layla said. "If you hadn't had an idol of success, you could have just shown him what you had done. Instead, you 'laid in wait' to see if he would notice it on his own."

"Showing him would sort of have defeated the purpose, wouldn't it?" Chloe asked.

"You mean the purpose of seeing if he was cooperating in honoring your idols?" Layla responded with a smile.

"If I have to tell him, it's not the same," Chloe protested. "It's like begging for appreciation."

"Your husband thought he was just coming home, but he was actually walking right into the middle of a sacrificial ceremony—*your* sacrificial ceremony to the idol of success. He had no idea he was expected to play a role in honoring that idol by offering appreciation and affirmation."

"Are you saying it was all my fault?"

"No, but we only have your side of what happened, and *your* heart to hear. With a God-pleasing heart motivation, the story would have sounded very different and ended very differently, too."

"At dinner, I was giving him the silent treatment," Chloe admitted. "I wanted him to know I was mad."

"You were trying to please yourself by expressing your dissatisfaction with his failure to honor your idol. When you sat with him in a loving way, you switched over to trying to please God—at least that's what I heard when you shared it."

"Yes, I really was trying to be God-pleasing when I did that. But then the thing with our son happened. That just sort of set me off again."

"And you switched back to trying to get what you wanted or thought you needed. You were trying to Control for Success by pretending to ignore your son's calls."

"I guess that's true."

"Success, in your mind, would have been for your husband to take responsibility for your son at that moment, or at least show appreciation for all you do, even when everything isn't perfect, right? Maybe having your husband's appreciation became the idol at that point. When he didn't respond as you desired, the 'goddess of your idol' raged that he wasn't worshipping as you required."

"I really feel that in my heart, when you say it like that."

"I honestly don't think helping your son would have bothered you much, if you hadn't been in idolatry."

"Probably not."

"You would have just done what needed to be done or said something like, 'I need you to take care of him tonight,' or, 'I need a break, will you help him?'"

"Why did he criticize me later, though?"

"I don't know," Layla said. "I'm sure he has his own heart issues; but he's not here, you are. Why did you go upstairs?"

"Because I was really angry and hurt. I couldn't stand being around him."

"In other words, when your first efforts didn't work, you took a more dramatic approach—something neither of you had ever done before—to try to get him to understand the seriousness of not participating in worshipping your idol."

"It sounds foolish when you put it that way."

"Trying to control for what you want and letting your worship of idolatrous desires determine your decisions is always destructive. The idol of your heart to feel competent and successful or the idol of wanting your husband's appreciation—

whichever you were worshipping at the time—led you to make decisions that actually resulted in the opposite."

"True," she said with a sigh.

"If you hadn't been worshipping those things, you could have simply said you were struggling with some things. Then you could have calmly and clearly explained your frustration and shared your heart—just as you shared it with us."

"I guess I really messed up."

"God always uses our mistakes to His glory; and when we confess our sins and turn our hearts back to Him, we are blessed by that glory. You've learned a lot from this about how your heart works and how destructive idolatry is, which is good. You won't be perfect until Christ perfects you at the last day, but the next time you have an idol you may be able to see it more easily and act more quickly."

"Thank you."

"All I've done is help you put things in a biblical perspective, and translate what you said into terms of worship and idolatry."

"I feel so at peace now, it's amazing," Chloe said.

☙ ❧

The symptoms of idolatry are painful, but God has put them in place as warnings signs or "caution flags,"[11] to get us to slow down, see we're headed in the wrong direction, and turn around. They are actually a blessing, because without them, we would have a clear path to destruction. Ignoring them means continuing in sin and rebellion, with the resulting burden of guilt that is worse than all other negative feelings combined.

5. The Symptoms

There are also evidences or symptoms that we are on the right side of the chart, with a heart truly seeking to please God. They are the peace *of* God, peace *with* God that comes from a pure conscience, a desire to obey God, and *all* the fruit of the Spirit . . . regardless of the circumstances.

> *Do not be anxious about anything, but in every situation, by prayer and petition, with thanksgiving, present your requests to God. And the* ***peace of God, which transcends all understanding****, will guard your hearts and your minds in Christ Jesus (Philippians 4:6-7).*
>
> *Since we have been justified by faith, we have* ***peace with God*** *through our Lord Jesus Christ (Romans 5:1) (Hebrews 9:14).*
>
> *If you love Me, you will* ***keep My commandments*** *(John 14:15).*
>
> *The* ***fruit of the Spirit*** *is love, joy, peace, forbearance, kindness, goodness, faithfulness, gentleness and self-control (Galatians 5:22-23).*

These verses are not prescriptions for *how* to set our hearts on God, but descriptions of what it looks like when our hearts *already are* set on Him. Trying to be peaceful, patient, loving, kind, self-disciplined, etc. so we can call ourselves godly is a bit like putting on colorful clothes and perfume, so we can call ourselves a flower. The blessings of God come from God, through faith in Jesus Christ, not through our own efforts.

In any situation, therefore, we can know whether or not our heart is truly worshipping God, by asking ourselves four simple questions. If the answer to even one of them is "no," some part of our heart is worshipping something else:

1. Right now, do I have the peace *of* God?
2. Right now, am I at peace *with* God?
3. Right now, do I *desire* to obey God, with joy?
4. Right now, do I have *all* the fruit of the Spirit?

☙ ❧

Complete the Idols Chart, by adding the symptoms of a Self-pleasing heart to the left side and evidence of a God-pleasing heart to the right. Draw a horizontal line just above the heart on the left side, to represent a one-way mirror to serve as a reminder of how difficult it is to see inside your own heart.

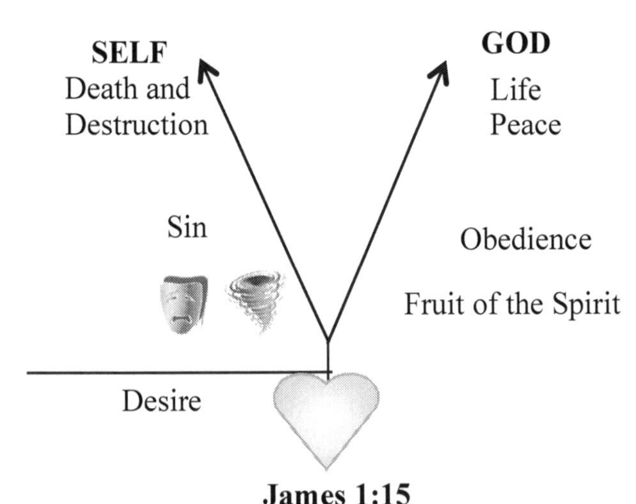

James 1:15

Desire when it has conceived gives birth to sin, and sin when it is full-grown, brings forth death.

CB 80

Idolatry is foundational to all other sins because it is a direct violation of the biblical command foundational to all other commands: *"I am the Lord your God, you shall have no other Gods before Me . . . for I, the Lord your God, am a jealous God" (Deuteronomy 5:7, 9).* Idolatry angers God (Deuteronomy 32:21), causes Him to turn His face away (Acts 7:42), remove His blessing (Ezekiel 11:21), and refuse to hear our prayers (Psalm 66:18, Isaiah 59:2). He doesn't do this out of cruelty, but so that His people will recognize the emptiness and destruction of life without Him, realize the powerlessness of their idols, and return to Him for the sake of His holy name (Ezekiel 36:22, 32).

> *Then you will call upon me and come and pray to me, and I will hear you. You will seek me and find me, when you seek me with all your heart (Jeremiah 29:12-13).*

> *Return to me, says the Lord of hosts, and I will return to you (Zechariah 1:3).*

> *Draw near to God, and He will draw near to you. Cleanse your hands, you sinners, and purify your hearts, you double-minded (James 4:8).*

You might say, "He'd catch more flies with honey," but we all tend to slip into greater dependence on ourselves, not God, when things are going well. Fortunately, He is always near (Acts 17:27-28), and nothing can separate us from His love as expressed in Christ. We need only seek Him with *all* our heart and soul, and we will find Him (Deuteronomy 4:29).

If you're thinking, *"Great, one more thing I have to do to be good enough for God,"* let that thought lead you to the understanding that you can *never* be good enough in your own strength. Be amazed as you come to know how ridiculously sinful your heart truly is—and then rejoice God knew it first.

> *I am sure that neither death nor life, nor angels nor rulers, **nor things present nor things to come,** nor powers, nor height nor depth, nor anything else in all creation, will be able to separate us from the love of God in Christ Jesus our Lord (Romans 8:38-39, emphasis added)*

☙ ❧☙ ❧

Note: The completed idols chart, with comprehensive notes for counseling reference is available in an 8 ½" x 11" laminated card format at www.godempowered.com.

Chapter 5 ~ Homework

1. When did you most recently have a downcast face and/or a tormenting spirit?

2. List the four evidences of a heart set on pleasing God:

3. Which fruit of the Spirit do you most often lack?

4. Search scripture to consider the difference between "peace *with* God" and "peace *of* God."

Chapter 5 ~ Prayer

Lord God,

The world is full of trouble and sorrow, but You give comfort and joy. Who can discern their own errors? Reveal and cleanse me of the hidden sins of my heart and keep me from willful sin (Psalm 19:12-13). Fill me with forgiveness for those whose lives have stirred anything in my heart that was displeasing to You, and give me thankfulness for whatever in me has been revealed. May I lean on Your strength when I am weak, rest in Your comfort when I am sad, stand on Your wisdom when I am confused, and be filled with Your peace when I am worried. I praise You, the Father of compassion and God of comfort, who comforts me in all my troubles, so that I can comfort those in any trouble, with the comfort I received from You (2 Corinthians 1:3-4). In the name of Jesus Christ, amen.

Journal

Draw an Idols Chart, with the desire related to the issue you chose to explore in this study to the left of the heart. Halfway up the chart on the left side, list some behaviors that have come out of that desire. At the top left, list some of the destructive consequences or heartaches that have resulted from those behaviors.

6. The Idols Test

Learning to identify the presence of an idol in your heart begins with noticing when you are lacking the peace *of* God, peace *with* God, the fruit of the Spirit, and the desire to obey God. Even before you start trying to figure out the specific idol, you can reduce the amount of destruction will cause by asking yourself this question:

> **How can I be pleasing to God—this moment, right now—no matter how painful the past, how frightening the present, and how impossible the future might seem?**

It's still important to identify the desire that has become your idol for the problem at hand, and the best time to do that is while you are still upset. It's just too hard once you feel in control again.

The "Idols Test" is a set of six fill-in-the-blank statements or questions that will help you get started in identifying an idol of the heart. You don't have to answer all six, if you find one or two most helpful. I tend to use the first one when examining my own heart, but I listen for all six when helping other people.

The Idols Test[12]

1. "If only________________, then I'd be happy."

This is my personal favorite of all the questions, the one I most often ask myself, and what I'm always listening for when helping someone else. Other versions might include: *"If only______, then I'd have peace," or, "If only_______, then I'd be satisfied with God's goodness."*

When considering a tragedy or a deep regret, it might be helpful to word this statement slightly differently. For example: *"If only I hadn't _____, I would be happy"; "If only ______ hadn't happened, I wouldn't be so angry at God"; or, "If only I knew _______ would (or would not) happen, I could have peace."* The goal is simply to try and identify what one thing you believe you most need in order to "be okay."

> *My people shall be satisfied with My goodness, declares the LORD (Jeremiah 31:14).*

2. "After all I've done, you would think___________."

This is like saying, *"After all I've sacrificed . . .."* Jesus' death put an end to all sacrifice except: the sacrifice of praise; the sacrifice of a contrite heart; and the living sacrifice of your body, holy and acceptable to God. Any other sacrifice, even a godly-sounding one—if made to get what you desire or protect against what you fear—is a sacrifice to an idol.

The sacrifices of God are a broken spirit; a broken and contrite heart, O God, You will not despise (Psalm 51:17).

Present your bodies as a living sacrifice, holy and acceptable to God, which is your spiritual worship (Romans 12:1).

Through [Jesus Christ] then let us continually offer up a sacrifice of praise to God, that is, the fruit of lips that acknowledge His name (Hebrews 13:15).

3. "What if __________?" "I'm afraid that ________."

Fear is worry for the future; and God says we should have no fear, except the worshipful fear of God. Another way to ask or state this might be: *"If only______, I wouldn't be so afraid."*

The LORD is on my side; I will not fear. What can man do to me? (Psalm 118:6).

The fear of man lays a snare, but whoever trusts in the Lord is safe (Proverbs 29:25).

Do not fear, for I am with you; do not be dismayed, for I am your God (Isaiah 41:10).

4. "I am entitled to__________________."

We're all sinners entitled to nothing but death, except for the salvation provided through the blood of Christ. Feeling entitled to anything is both self-righteous and idolatrous.

For all [who believe] have sinned and fall short of the glory of God, and are justified by his grace as a gift, through the redemption that is in Christ Jesus (Romans 3:23-24).

The wages of sin are death, but the free gift of God is eternal life in Christ Jesus our Lord (Romans 6:23).

5. "How do I get (someone) to (do or not do something)? "

This question typically involves concern for how someone else's decision or choices are affecting your peace or happiness. Trying to get someone to *stop* doing what they're doing, or start doing what you think they should do, usually means trying to control that person's sin, which you simply are not able to do.

There is one God, and there is one mediator between God and men, the man Christ Jesus (1 Timothy 2:5).

6. "I'm willing to sin, in order to _________,"[13] or "I'm wiling to sin, if _________________."

Since idolatry always leads to sin, and sin is always a sign of idolatry, being willing to sin in *order to get* what you want or willing to sin if you *don't* get what you want are reliable clues you are worshipping something other than God.

You shall worship the Lord your God, and Him only shall you serve (Luke 4:8).

6. "I really wish I had handled ________differently."

I added this question as the result of learning first-hand that hidden regrets, even those that are not sinful, can make us defensive, hard-hearted, and resistant to the Holy Spirit.

> *Let the wicked forsake his way, and the unrighteous man his thoughts; let him return to the Lord, that He may have compassion on him, and to our God, for He will abundantly pardon (Isaiah 55:7).*

ଓ ଛ

The following areas of our heart provide fertile ground for idolatry. That doesn't mean they are idols of your heart now, but they could easily become some. Try to write a meaningful answer for each suggestion below.

Something you want to attain or gain.

Something you worry or think about a lot.

Something you are afraid will happen (or never happen).

Something you want to be right about.

Some way you want someone else to change.

Something you wish had never happened to you.

Something you wish you hadn't done, or had done.

Something about someone that makes your life difficult.

Something you worry people may think of you.

Something that makes you feel afraid or helpless.

Something that makes you feel defensive or jealous.

Something you feel you deserve.

☙ ❧

Some desires (or fears) are more difficult to recognize as potential idols than others. Long-standing *guilt* or *regret,* for example, can be an idolatrous effort of the heart to atone for a past wrongdoing or warn and remind yourself not to repeat a particular mistake. Long-standing *fear* or *shame* can be an idolatrous effort to protect against further harm from trauma, tragedy, disaster, or abuse. I don't say that flippantly, as though a hurting person should just "let it all go" and pretend they aren't in pain, but it is important to be able to identify and relinquish any related idols in order to experience the healing and peace only God can provide.

It's also worth mentioning that even godly-sounding desires, such as wanting your spouse to know the Lord, have a successful ministry, build a large church, or "be godly," can become idols of the heart that lead to sinful and destructive behavior. I was guilty of this in the previous chapter when I disregarded my husband and my marriage for the sake of editing a chapter or two of this book. It's no surprise that whatever I wrote under those circumstances inevitably ended up having to be rewritten.

☙ ❧

In the following story, try to identify the evidence of idolatry in Aesha's heart, as she contemplates the impact of having a child on her and her husband's life:

Aesha held the pregnancy test stick between her fingers, mentally rehearsing all the things she would say to her husband when he got home. The good news was that she was pregnant. The bad news was that they couldn't afford a baby on her husband's salary. He would have to ask for a raise, or she would have to stop going to college and get a job, maybe even quit the program entirely—at least until the baby was in school.

They had had a discussion about her quitting school when the car needed repairs, and another time when they had some unexpected bills, but they had managed to pay those off. A baby was altogether different. The numbers just didn't work.

She knew he would balk at asking for a raise. Every time she brought it up, he said he didn't want to and that he would surely get one at the next review. He did, but it was always a meager amount. She didn't want to quit college with less than a year left, and she didn't want to delay by going part time. He *had* to ask for a raise.

Later that evening, Aesha's husband was thrilled when she told him about the pregnancy, but he knew the awkward silence following their celebratory hug meant she was going to talk about his salary again. "Don't," he said. "I know what you're going to say and the answer is no, I'm not going to ask."

"Not even for our baby?" Aesha asked incredulously. "I know you're scared, but I am, too. If I quit school now, how will we ever have enough in the future to raise this child? We can't do it on what you make now. You *have* to ask for a raise. Tell them we're having a baby. Why won't you do that for me? Why won't you do it for *us?"* she asked.

"I can't push my luck. They're laying people off and if I lose my job it will be even worse. God will provide for us, I'm sure. Don't worry."

"And if He doesn't? You have no idea how hard it is to feed just the two of us on our budget. I'm stressed, and stress isn't good for the baby. I knew I should have never started school—I could have been working all this time and putting the money aside for a house. Now we'll never get out of this apartment."

"Don't quit. I'm telling you we will be fine. Finish your degree and you'll see."

"But what about when the baby comes? Then what?

"It's going to be fine," her husband said as he reached toward her.

Pulling away, Aesha fumed. "You always say that."

"Hasn't God always seen us through?" he asked.

"Yes, but that doesn't mean He will this time. Maybe He doesn't want me to get a degree. Maybe this is a sign. What if he wants me to, but I can't? I'm so confused. If we get evicted, then what? Are we going to move in with your dad and admit we can't take care of ourselves? What if you lose your job? We could end up living out of our car like Maggie and Phil. I think I'm going to be sick."

Walking back to the kitchen, Aesha stared at the textbooks spread out on the table. She should have been studying for the next day's exam, but she couldn't concentrate. Tears filled her eyes as she wondered why God had given her such a stubborn husband. Why was he so afraid? Didn't he love her and the baby enough to fight for what he deserved?

Both Aesha and her husband wanted financial stability and the ability to provide for their child. Her husband was able to hold that desire with an open hand before God, but Aesha had made an idol of it. Asking for a raise was the offering she wanted her husband to make to that idol; and when he refused, she was hurt and angry.

Aesha loved God, but she was putting her trust for the future in something other than God. Having an idol-free heart didn't mean she couldn't plan for the future or still encourage her husband to ask for a raise; but there was a big difference between striving for those things with a heart fixed on her own fears and longings, and a heart fixed on pleasing God.

☙ ❧

A common mistake people make when trying to identify an idol of their heart is calling the *object* of their desire their idol. For example, they might say, "Joe is my idol." Worshipping a physical thing or person *is* a form of idolatry, but in order to correctly identify the *idol of the heart* you have to identify the underlying motivation for that wrong worship.

For example, the Israelites worshipped a physical idol when in the desert; but the motivation for their physical idolatry was a desire to return to Egypt. That was the *idol of their heart* and hope for the future. Making offerings and sacrifices to the physical idol was just the means by which they hoped to satisfy that heart idol (Exodus 32).

The best way to avoid this confusion is to see if desire you think is your idol will fit, grammatically speaking, in the first "Idols Test" statement:

"If only_______, then I'd be happy (or have peace)."

By testing "Joe" as an idol in that phrase you can see it would be grammatically incorrect to say, *"If only Joe, then I'd be happy."* Therefore, Joe is not an idol of the heart.

However, *"If only Joe liked me, I'd be happy,"* or, *"If only I could be like Joe, I'd be happy,"* are grammatically correct sentences. Therefore, wanting Joe to like you or wanting to be like Joe, could be idols of your heart.

The difference is crucial. Freedom from wrong worship will not come from confessing "Joe" as an idol. It will only come from correctly confessing the underlying idolatrous desires regarding Joe. In the same way, confessing "a new house" as an idol is not the same as confessing "the *desire* for a new house."

Likewise, "life" as a concept is not generally an idol, but "living a long and healthy life" is a common idol most of us share. You must identify the *desire* to which you are holding your happiness hostage, in order to accurately confess the idol. Your happiness and security must rest in God alone.

6. The Idols Test

ଓ ଃ

Idols often come in layers—like Russian nesting dolls, with one hidden inside another, those two inside a third, etc.—so that your deepest and most cherished desires are protected beneath layers of other, less significant ones. The fact that one or more might sound godly only adds to the difficulty of recognizing them.

For example, over a period of many years, I had tried to relinquish an idol of wanting my husband to stop certain behaviors I knew were displeasing to God—and to me. Over and over, I confessed the desire for him to stop as an idol, but I never experienced God's lasting peace. Anger and hurt still consumed me every time I saw him do what I hated.

One day, God showed me that wanting him to stop was a superficial idol hiding a deeper idol of wanting to be able to *control* my husband's sin. My inability to do so upset me even more than his behavior—which explained why sometimes it didn't bother me much at all, while other times it drove me into a quiet rage. I couldn't be my husband's Holy Spirit, no matter how hard I tried. *That* was the real root of my pain and anger.

Freedom didn't come from throwing up my hands and giving up or pretending not to care. Nor did it come from adopting a martyr's quiet self-righteousness. It came from confessing the idolatrous desire of wanting to be able to control my husband's sin.

The behavior still mattered and I still cared; but in a God-pleasing way, rather than a self-pleasing one. There was no longer anxiety, worry, snooping, anger, or fear—a transformation of heart so dramatic it could not have been explained or accomplished by any willful means. All those feelings were simply gone and remain so to this day.

As is often the case with confessed idolatry, God also began working in my husband's heart, drawing him close and convicting him in ways I had never been able. I still pray for him, but with confident trust that God is in control and desires even more than I do for him to love and honor the Lord. My joy in our marriage no longer depends on my husband changing, for God has given me true contentment.

We rarely have any difficulties now, and our home is a peaceful, loving one. There are frustrations from time to time, of course, but even those are infrequent. When they arise, my first response now is to stop and consider how I can be pleasing to God in the situation—rather than wish God would change my husband so it would easier for me to be more God-pleasing.

☙ ❧

In order to identify which is the primary or underlying idol of the heart and which are supporting or protecting ones, imagine each desire in turn being satisfied, while all the others stay the same. Say there is a potential promotion you want very much. Given your longing to be selected, sacrifices made to gain that recognition, and anxiousness to know the decision you might conclude you have made an idol of the desire for a promotion.

Putting that desire in the first Idols Test question, you would say, *"If only I could get that promotion, I would be happy."* Since that is a grammatically correct statement, you might then confess the desire for a promotion as an idol and ask

God to remove it. If your fears are replaced by calm clarity and peace, you likely diagnosed the idol of your heart correctly.

What if there is no peace, though? What if, even after sincerely confessing repenting of the desire for a promotion as an idol, you still feel anxious? It is possible, then, that the *desire for greater respect and influence in the company* is the deeper idol, and "being promoted" is just the means by which you hope to gain that respect or influence.

It's just as possible, however, for the opposite to be true: that *being promoted* is the primary idol of the heart, and having greater respect and influence is the superficial idol set up as the critical means by which to accomplish that goal. In other words, you might be worshipping the desire for greater respect, but it's in service to the *real* idol of wanting to be promoted.

You can test these possibilities to see which is true, by comparing them one against the other:

> If the promotion came, **but the respect (or ability to influence) didn't**, would I be happy?

Then in reverse:

> If my boss respected me (or I had influence), **but someone else received the promotion**, would I be happy?

If considering the first possibility gives you the most peace, then the primary idol is probably "being promoted." If the second one gives you the most peace, then the primary idol is probably "being respected or having influence."

Comparing desires like this is especially helpful in situations where it is difficult to think clearly because of the risk of making a wrong decision. The true story of a father struggling with his daughter's self-harm is an excellent example of how to apply this concept in real-life.

☙ ❧

When Christopher first found out his daughter was cutting herself, he was stunned. She had always been the "good girl" of his two daughters—respectful at home, responsible at school, and serving as a worship leader in the church youth group.

Emily told her dad that she didn't really know why she started self-harming. She had heard of other kids doing it, looked it up on the Internet, tried it, and found it helped relieve her stress. She admitted she knew it wasn't God pleasing and said she had already stopped. It wasn't long however, before Christopher found out she had just learned to hide the evidence better.

Christopher tried "giving the situation to God," but had come to realize that effort was more an exercise in trying not to worry, than an act of worship. Despite his prayers, God's supernatural peace was not consistently and powerfully present, and it seemed like Emily was slipping away.

Over several days, Christopher asked himself the Idols Test questions and made a list of possible idols: wanting Emily to stop self-harming, wanting to be a positive influence in her life, wanting her to respect him as her father, wanting her to love God, wanting her to care about her health, wanting her to be safe, and others. He then reduced those down to just a few by comparing and contrasting to see which it seemed would give him the most peace.

In the end, he settled on two primary desires: for Emily to stop self-harming and for her to grow in her knowledge and love of God. In the past, this is where he would have stopped, for both desires seemed good. This time, he went on to check those desires for idolatry and identify which was the primary idol of his heart, by asking himself this important question:

> *Would I have more peace if my daughter knew God, but still kept harming herself; or if she stopped harming herself, but still didn't know God?*

Christopher could tell by the response of his heart that even though he certainly *did* want his daughter to grow in knowledge and love of the Lord, his underlying motivation for that desire—at the moment—was hope that a stronger faith would cause her to stop self-harming. Recognizing "getting Emily to stop" was the core idol, he confessed that desire as an idol and asked God to remove it from his heart.

It was a terrifying request, because for months he had emotionally and spiritually clung to his hopes for Emily. Asking for that desire to be removed felt like giving permission for her to continue—even blessing it. He worried God might think he didn't care whether she ever got well or not. As long as he was confessing that desire out of conviction idolatry was a sin against God, rather than out of hope that *now* his daughter would stop harming herself, he had no need to fear.

As soon as Christopher repented of his idolatry, the tormenting spirit of confusion and calculating desire to Control for Success disappeared, and he had the inexplicable peace of God. He was able to speak openly and honestly with Emily, ask questions without fearing her answers, guide her in learning to examine her own heart, and give her wisdom for struggling with sin. His worry and fears no longer clouded their communication, and his prayers were no longer pleas for God to serve his desires for his daughter. They became true intercessions on her behalf.

"I am not afraid anymore," Christopher said as he shared his testimony with our small group. "I know this is Emily's struggle with sin, between her and God; and I can see God is working in her heart. I bear the burden of a parent, but that burden is reflected in prayer now, rather than in efforts to control. Our conversations are calm discussions about how faith and life intersect in temptation and sin—not on how she needs to change her behavior."

Today, Emily has a father she can go to who is not threatened by the dangers of her sin, nor trying to control her. He is helping her understand the spiritual truths God is demonstrating through her struggle—something that will serve her well for the rest of her life. Her cutting has steadily diminished, and her love of the Lord is becoming more and more evident. Should she ever fully turn to God in this area of her life, it will be a testimony to His glory—but not more so than the supernatural peace God has given her father already.

Someone in the group later asked: "You said God never blesses our idols. What if Emily's mother still had an idol in her heart for her to stop cutting, when the father relinquished his?

Wouldn't that mean God blessed the mother's idol, when Emily stopped cutting and sought to please God more?"

It was an interesting question, one that led to an important point. Learning to identify and confess idols is *not* about gaining a new technique for controlling the future or getting someone to change, but about having God's peace in all circumstances. The person whose heart is turned to God will *always* be blessed by Him, whether or not the circumstances *ever* change. Conversely, the person who remains in idolatry will never be truly satisfied or at peace—even if everything they desire comes to pass.

Two years later, I reached out to Emily and her father for an update. When I learned she was doing well, I asked her to reflect back and tell me a bit about what had been going on during that difficult period of her life.

Emily replied she had accepted Christ at a church retreat during middle school and had been very happy in her faith for the first few years. In high school, however, she had become keenly aware of her heart's ability to sin and had tried to control those inclinations by diligently reading her Bible every day, setting strict behavioral rules for herself, and taking on leadership roles in student ministry.

The more everyone thought she was "a good Christian girl," however, the more she felt she was living a lie. Hopelessness and a sense of failure grew into rebellion, and her love of Christ grew dim. She even began to doubt her salvation. Self-harm, she said, was an effort to try and find relief, but it was only temporary and was always followed by waves of even worse guilt and depression.

Unbeknownst to her parents or me, Emily had become preoccupied with thoughts of suicide. More than once, she planned steps to kill herself, but something always interfered—which she now attributes to God. At the time, however, those interferences only added to her feelings of failure and led her to try other forms of self-harm.

In the few times I visited with Emily, I had tried to help her understand that struggling with sin was normal. Being a Christian wasn't about trying to be perfect, I had assured her, but about drawing nearer to Christ in our imperfection. Looking back, she said, those conversations had helped, but she had been determined not to admit it. A friend's comment that "no one can out-sin God" was the key that began to soften her heart.

The turning point came when Emily realized her parents—who had stopped worshipping their desire for her to change—were no longer frightened by her sin. Their previous efforts to be perfect had not been the example they hoped. They had only made Emily feel more rebellious, sinful, and unlovable in contrast. When she began to see that her sin was not greater than God's ability to give her parents peace, she began to want that peace for herself.

Then, one morning, Emily suddenly woke to find the joy of the Lord restored in her heart. Miraculously, inexplicably, the depression and desire to self-harm were gone, and the peace of God filled her heart. Today, she is living a life of confident faith, much wiser than she once was about what it means to seek to please God. She is once again serving in the church with joy, and her relationship with her parents is growing in love and respect.

ଓ ଔ

When there are many different desires to weigh, you can compare them by starting with two, deciding which would give the greater peace, then carrying that one forward to compare with the next desire. Alternatively, you could just consider each one in relation to all the others:

> **If** (a particular desire) **came about, but nothing else changed, would I be okay** (or able to handle everything else)?
>
> Or, in undesirable circumstances:
>
> **If I knew** (a particular fear) **would never happen, but nothing else changed, would I be okay now** (or able to handle everything else)?

I used this approach when helping Amy, a former missionary, examine her heart's confusion and anxiety about what she called her "shortcomings." Amy had always been drawn to missionary work and excitedly accepted her first long-term assignment right after college. In the field, however, she found her peers less concerned about pleasing God than she thought they should be, and her reluctance to participate in certain behaviors left her feeling isolated and judged.

Upon returning home, Amy took a full-time job with a social services organization, where she greatly enjoyed working with clients and having a steady income. Promoted to a higher-paying position with virtually no client contact and more responsibility than she was comfortable handling, she tried to explain her disappointment and sense of inadequacy to her boss; but it didn't go well.

Trying to decide whether to stick it out in the new position, ask for her old job back, look for a new job, or return to the mission field, Amy diligently searched scripture and prayed. When we met, she shared conflicting thoughts about a life-long desire to be a missionary, lingering anger and disappointment over her first missionary assignment, guilt for having left the mission field, enjoyment of the business world, frustration in the new position, and anxiety about trying to get her boss' support and understanding.

I assured Amy I didn't know which, if any, of those desires might be an idol of her heart, but I could ask questions that might help her figure it out or open the door for God to show her. Since she kept returning in conversation to the mission field incident, I began by asking, "If that had never happened, would you be okay right now?"

"No, I would still be upset about the current situation and not know what to do."

We tested each of the different desires she had mentioned—asking if it was satisfied, but nothing else changed, would she be okay—but none stood out as more significant than the others. Unsure of what to say next, I tried rephrasing the original question. "How do you think your life might be different now, if the earlier event in the mission field had never happened?"

"I'm terrified God will put me in another position where I'll feel abandoned or unsupported," Amy replied. It was not a direct answer to my question, but it had come unfiltered from her heart and even startled her when she said it. She wasn't sure whether God might put her in a similar position as punishment or providence, but she immediately recognized the error of putting more trust in that fear than in God's goodness.

"What if you knew nothing like that would ever happen again?" I asked. "Would you then feel you could handle what is happening now?"

"Yes," she said. "If I knew my boss would understand and support me, I could talk to her; but I am feeling judged and rejected again for just being me.

When I pointed out the connection between the fear of being judged and the desire for acceptance and approval, Amy easily recognized the roots of pride. Even her effort to be godly was an offering or sacrifice to an idol, when that effort was motivated by the desire to avoid criticism. Confessing these things, Amy felt God's peace and was able to calmly speak about the situation with her boss, while biblically evaluating her options—without the confusion of wrong worship.

I spoke to Amy recently, now many months removed from our first conversation, and was struck by how much her faith had matured. She had decided to stay in her new job for a while to help see the organization through some major projects, but she was in the process of leaving and seeking to do so in the most God-pleasing way possible.

⁂

Once an idol of the heart has been identified and confessed, there is no more defensiveness, no need to rehearse different scenarios or anticipate objections, no self-righteousness, no urge to control, and little concern about how other people's sins affect you. There is just God's peace. It is difficult to imagine what that's like, until you've experienced it.

The most striking change when your heart is made pure, however, is a sudden lack of anxiety about the future. Given the very human habit of Controlling for Success, this may seem impossible to imagine—even foolish or irresponsible. We are more accustomed to asking God to help us achieve what we want, than leaving the outcome completely to Him, especially considering how His ways often seem at odds with our own.

When drawing near to the house of God, the Bible says, it is better to listen than speak, *for a fool's voice comes with many words.* We aren't even to let *our hearts* toil and spin with dreams or thoughts about what we want to happen, for it's all just efforts to control.

> *Guard your steps when you go to the house of God. To draw near to listen is better than to offer the sacrifice of fools, for they do not know that they are doing evil.*
>
> *Be not rash with your mouth, nor let your heart be hasty to utter a word before God, for God is in heaven and you are on earth.*
>
> *Therefore let your words be few. For a dream comes with much business, and a fool's voice with many words (Ecclesiastes 5:1-3).*

Surely if we are to remember God's sovereignty in our interactions with Him, by letting our words be few, we are to remember it no less in our interactions with one another. We can do that by stating the facts of a situation in as few words as possible—and then being quiet and waiting for a response, before speaking again. I call this form of communication "The Art of the Awkward Silence," because it feels so awkward to *not* keep talking.

The Art of the Awkward Silence

Practicing the Art of the Awkward Silence is not hard, except for the temptation to continue talking. It is as simple as stating the facts of a situation or problem in as few words as possible *("Be not rash with your mouth . . . for God is in heaven and you are on earth . . . therefore, let your words be few,")* then stopping and waiting. A somewhat humorous tool I use whenever I'm tempted to keep on talking is to wait a number of seconds equal to the age of the person I'm talking to before I speak again.

Women tend to be less comfortable with pauses in conversation and first to rush to fill those pauses with explanations, accusations, rationalizations, manipulations, expectations, justifications, solutions, or self-defenses. However, we would *all* do well—men and women alike—to remember that trying to control other people with our words is still trying to Control for Success, and not at all what God calls us to do.

It's important to remember that the Art of the Awkward Silence is not a matter of clenching our teeth, biting our tongue, or self-righteously assuming God will "correct" the other person. Nor is it a psychological gimmick, a clever tool for effective communication, or a way to get someone else to do or say what we want. It's simply a matter of resisting trying to control with our words and leaving room for God to move in the conversation—and the problem at hand—rather than acting as though He couldn't possibly have anything to add that we haven't already thought of ourselves.

> *Do you see someone who is hasty in their words? There is more hope for a fool than for that person (from Proverbs 29:20).*

☙ ❧

Some examples of stating a problem as simply as possible and leaving room for the Holy Spirit to provide a solution could be:

"The disposal stopped working." <wait>
"The trash is overflowing. <wait>
"This room is a mess." <wait>
"The bills have to be paid tomorrow." <wait>
"John failed his chemistry class." <wait>
"We are arguing an awful lot these days." <wait>
"We haven't spent much time together lately." <wait>
"This show is too difficult for me to watch." <wait>
"I'm exhausted." <wait>
"I'm not comfortable with that." <wait>

Another example is stating a solution or summary, leaving room for the Holy Spirit to move in the other person to influence the next steps:

"We need to leave by 7:30." <wait>
"The trash needs to be put out." <wait>
"An allowance is a privilege, not a right." <wait>
"I'd like do something together this week." <wait>
"We need to pray about this." <wait>
"There is a tutor available this week." <wait>
"I would like to hire someone to help clean. <wait >
"We need to talk." <wait>
(To a child) "The street is for cars, not children." <wait>
"We can't keep tearing each other down." <wait>
"I need to rest." <wait>

Always avoid global judgments or generalizations, such as, "You always __________," or "You are so __________." These types of statements treat others as the sum of their worst character traits or behaviors and are extremely self-righteous. Instead, assume the best of them, treating troublesome behavior as a specific, separate issue—just as you would want God to do with you. Some ways to convey this might be:

"That wasn't like you." <wait>
"That was inappropriate (hurtful, etc.)" <wait>
"You don't seem yourself lately." <wait>
"Something must be troubling you." <wait>
"It was surprising that you _______." <wait>

Express emotions in simple, factual statements, rather than take on the role of the Holy Spirit in trying to convict others to repentance. Be a living testimony of faith by not pretending to "have it all together" or never struggling with sin. Share your desire to please God, even in times of difficulty.

"I am deeply hurt." <wait>
"Words cannot express my pain." <wait>
"This is really difficult for me" <wait>
"I was offended by what you said." <wait>
"That was not God-honoring." <wait>
"I felt unloved when_____." <wait>
"This is not going well." <wait>
"Right now, I find it hard to trust you." <wait>
"I am not comfortable with that." <wait>

Be a living testimony of faith by not pretending to "have it all together" or never struggle with sin. Share your desire to please God, even in times of difficulty:

"I am having trouble feeling loving right now." <wait>
"I'm not sure how to honor God in this." <wait>
"I am struggling to trust God in this." <wait>
"I need to ask your forgiveness." <wait>
"I need your prayers." <wait>
"I have a confession to make." <wait>
"I have to pray about this before responding." <wait>
"I want to please God in this, but I'm scared." <wait>
"I feel we're focusing on what we want to see happen, rather than on honoring God." <wait>

You can apply these principles to phone calls, e-mails, and text as easily as face-to-face interaction. Just remember to keep the communication short and simple, present only one factual statement or problem at a time, and don't fixate on a particular solution in advance. Don't try to anticipate every counterpoint or strive for a preconceived result as though your life depended on it.

Conversations are so much more godly and complete when you stop trying to control through your words. They become like a dance, with God providing the music, and each person responding in turn—even when the other person isn't a believer.

☙ ❧

The following true story demonstrates how letting your words be few—because God is in heaven and you are on earth—can help you talk with someone about an issue, even before you have fully identified the idol in your own heart. It's possible God may even keep you from seeing your heart clearly in order that you will address a particular issue. Just be sure to leave room for Him in the conversation, by stating the facts simply and waiting before speaking again.

When Clara learned her husband had given money to his parents again without telling her, she was furious. She wanted to address the matter calmly and wisely, but found it hard to get past the anger and bitterness she felt.

Recognizing the symptoms of idolatry, she tried to figure out if she was upset because her husband gave his parents money, the fact that he did so without asking or telling her, the impact it would have on their finances, her own insecurity that she was not contributing financially to the family income, or wanting her husband to understand how much he had hurt her.

Confused and overcome with hurt and anger, she typically would have expressed to those emotions by saying something like this:

> *I can't believe you gave your parents money without telling me, much less asking me! I had to hear it from your brother. Do you realize how embarrassing that was? I'm not even sure we can pay our own bills this month! Maybe we need it more than they do, did you think of that? And don't tell me it's "your money." Just because I don't work doesn't mean I don't have a say in our finances. Don't you ever do that again!*

On better days, she might have been able to control her emotions and explain her position calmly, with an appeal to her husband's conscience:

> *I'm not trying to be ugly about giving money to your parents, but it really hurts me when you do it without even talking to me about it. I don't think it's right, because we are a couple. We are one flesh, and it is our money. I want to honor them and help them, but it upsets me that you don't seem to even care what I think. I know I don't contribute to our family financially, but I still contribute in other ways and should have a say in how we spend our money.*
>
> *You know we need to get the air-conditioner fixed, and now we may not be able to. Hearing from someone else you have again given money to your parents without discussing it first is unbelievably*

painful. I have a right to be involved in these decisions. Have you even considered how we are going to pay to get the air conditioner fixed?

Either way, she would have been trying to control. He would have responded with self-justification and defensiveness, and she would have been doubly offended by his refusal to admit wrongdoing.

Instead, even though not yet able to identify her idol of the heart, she left room for God by stating the facts of the situation as simply as possible.

"I'm very hurt and angry," Clara said.

"Why?" her husband asked.

"I don't feel it's appropriate for you to give money to your parents without talking to me first," she said, stating another fact. She stopped speaking and waited.

"They needed it right away, and we had it," her husband said, after realizing she wasn't going to keep talking. "I don't know why it upsets you. They're my parents."

"That's not the point," Clara replied. She wanted to say more, but waited.

"It's money I earned, anyway," her husband continued.

Rather than respond defensively, Clara chose to reply to her husband's comment in terms of biblical truth. *"We are one flesh, and we each contribute to the marriage in meaningful ways,"* she said, feeling a shift in her heart. Speaking simply and factually was becoming easier.

Her husband didn't respond, and she resisted the temptation to explain or justify her feelings. She knew only the Holy Spirit could convict his conscience.

After waiting a bit, she simply said, "I don't mind helping your parents, but we need to be in agreement before doing so." Surprisingly, he didn't argue and he promised to discuss financial decisions in the future. It seemed like a miracle.

Less than a month later, he sidestepped that promise by being deceitful in *how* he discussed an investment he wanted to make. Clara was furious and no longer felt like pleasing God or examining her heart. It was too hard to think that wanting to be involved in the family's financial decisions could be an idol. Still, she practiced the Art of the Awkward Silence.

"This is completely unacceptable!" she exclaimed.

"What?" her husband asked, pretending not to know.

"You know exactly what I'm referring to," she said, letting her words be few and wondering what God might do.

"We talked about it and you said it was okay," he argued.

"You did *not* tell me it would use all of our savings or that my Dad was loaning you additional money for it!"

"It's no big deal."

"It's a very big deal. It is difficult to honor you as my husband when you lie to me," she said, stating a simple fact.

"You always complain," her husband said.

Ignoring his effort to deflect attention from the problem, Clara said, "This is the second time you have deceived me with regard to our finances." After a long pause, she added a testimony: "I am struggling to know how to respond in a God-pleasing manner to what you have done."

Her husband grumbled and left the room, and Clara resisted the temptation to let anger overtake her. She trusted

God would always provide for their needs, so she wasn't worried about the money. It was the way her husband—a man who loved God—had made the decision without her, breaking his promise and deceiving her to do so. Confessing she had made an idol of the not ungodly desire for him to include her in those decisions, she repented to God in her heart.

An hour later, her husband came back into the room, acknowledged his wrongdoing, and asked Clara's forgiveness. That night they went over their finances in detail, created a budget, and established agreement on the types and sizes of expenditures they would discuss with each other before making them. He shared his desires for the future and she shared hers, as they worked on establishing a common set of financial goals.

Tentatively, Clara then told her husband what she had learned about idols of the heart and asked him to pray that they would submit those financial goals to God and resist worshipping them. He agreed, and of his own accord asked God to help them glorify Him in all they did. That may seem inconsequential given his deceit, but it was significant to Clara that she could see God working in her husband's heart.

ଓ ଥ

Clara relied on Ecclesiastes 5:2 as a reminder to let her words be few, rather than explode in anger. The next story shows how Mariam, a pastor's wife, relied on the same verse to let her words be few in speaking up, rather than be silent.

Although Miriam knew her husband sincerely wanted to spend more time with her and the children, there was always something calling him away as the pastor of a small and growing church. Miriam wanted to tell her husband she needed him home more, but she was afraid it might lead him to make changes that would hurt the church or make the members angry. She worried he might even resent her for needing him so much or for not being supportive enough as a pastor's wife.

No matter how many times Miriam rehearsed what she might say to her husband, she couldn't imagine it ending well. So, instead, she tried to please God by praying and continuing to support her husband without complaint. Over time, however, she found herself becoming increasingly bitter and missing God's peace.

"Can you lay all those good, but seemingly conflicting desires—for your husband to serve God as a father and a pastor, for him to not be disappointed in you, and for him to keep doing what is important to him—before the Lord and leave them with Him?" I asked.

"Yes, but I feel like I'm going to go crazy if I don't say something," Mariam said.

"Maybe God is leading you to speak up. He knows your heart and could be working through you to help your husband in this area.

"But how do I know what to say?"

"Present the problem factually, without a solution, just the way you stated it to me: you want him home more, you want him to be happy in his ministry, and you want the church to grow. Then stop. You could add you are concerned he might feel pressured by your needs or disappointed in you, or that you are struggling to know how to please God in this situation. Just try to present the problem in as few words as possible and wait.

Leave room for God to move in the silence to provide His wisdom for you both.

"That sounds strange, but easy," she said.

"Learning to speak the truth of a problem without fear of the future is the easiest and most honest way to communicate, especially when you don't know the solution—and in this case, you really don't know."

"Thinking about it that way makes me feel like a huge burden has been lifted off my shoulders. It's so obvious. I've been trying hard to figure out the answer and do what was pleasing to God all this time, but even in my prayers for my husband, I can see I was trying to control."

Later that evening, Miriam spoke to her husband. "I am struggling because I want to have more time together as a family," she said, "but I also want you to fulfill your calling as a pastor." Then she was quiet.

Her husband began by acknowledging the challenges of being a pastor. He confessed he struggled with turning down requests from church members and feared putting his family's needs ahead of God's desires. Together they prayed, asking God for wisdom. Then, they put in writing God's commands for family and church, and looked at how they were honoring each.

Miriam began to realize how it honored God to let her husband know when she needed his time. Her husband began to realize how it honored God to have guidelines and boundaries for how he allocated his time.

☙ ❧

It's never too late to begin considering the possibility of an idol in your heart, no matter how long a situation has gone on or how much destruction has been caused by it. There isn't a "lesser blessing" God might give you today than He could have given you yesterday or last year. His blessings are always whole and complete, without regard to time.

The prospect of *not* having a particular idol might seem frightening, but God can calm the stormy seas in an instant (Matthew 8:23-27). So, regardless of your circumstances, ask Him for His wisdom (James 1:5). Confess your sins to one another (James 5:16) and pray—not to try to get God to listen, but because He *does* listen (Matthew 6:7-8). When you are too confused or upset to know how to pray, just be still and pray the prayer Jesus taught his disciples:

> *Our Father in heaven, hallowed be Your name. Your kingdom come, Your will be done, on earth as it is in heaven. Give us this day our daily bread and forgive us our debts, as we have forgiven our debtors. And lead us not into temptation, but deliver us from evil. [For Yours is the kingdom and the power and the glory forever. Amen]' (Matthew 6:9-13, with common ending.)*

If you are lacking in faith, ask Him for faith. If your love for someone has grown cold, ask Him to fill you with love for that person. If you are struggling to forgive, ask Him to fill you with a spirit of forgiveness. If you are weak, ask Him for strength. If you are afraid, ask Him for peace and protection. If you are hungry, ask Him for food.

Resist the devil's temptations to dwell on the past, wish you could undo what was done, or go back and do things differently. Those feelings are just other idols. Set your heart fully on God today and move forward in as God-pleasing a manner as possible. He won't forget your past sin as though it never happened. He will turn it around and use it for His glory; and if your heart is set on Him, you will be blessed as He is glorified.

> *In love He predestined us for adoption as sons through Jesus Christ, according to the purpose of His will, to the praise of His glorious grace, with which He has blessed us in the Beloved (Ephesians 1:5-6).*

☙ ❧☙ ❧

Chapter 6 - Homework

1. What possible idols did you hear in Aesha's story? Restate them so they fit the first Idols Test question: *"If only_________, then she'd be happy."*

2. Think of a difficult situation you regularly face that often ends in argument or tension. Make a list of things you could say that are honest facts, spoken in as few words as possible:

3. Share what happened when you put the Art of the Awkward Silence into practice, using a few of the statements above.

4. What hinders you most when trying to apply the truths you have learned so far?

Chapter 6 ~ Prayer

Lord God,

I confess I have been worshipping an idol of ________. Remove that idol from my heart. Take it away and give me a clean heart that worships only You. Renew a right and willing spirit within me. Restore to me the joy of Your salvation (from Psalm 51:10, 12). I call to You in my distress, for I know You will answer me and give me strength (from Psalm 138:3). In Jesus' name, amen.

Journal

Each time you are anxious or upset this week, try expressing your feelings in the sentence, "If only __________, then I'd be happy (not anxious, at peace, etc.)" Look back over the desires you listed at the end of Chapter 2 or 4. How are these currently impacting your life?

7. The Challenge of Trust

Maura is a Bible teacher who loves Jesus and knows worshipping idols isn't godly, yet isn't convinced her own desires could be idolatrous. We've corresponded off and on for several years, and from time to time she has recognized the signs of idolatry in her heart; but she's only surrendered those desires intellectually, still clinging to the "right" to have them. In one of her notes, she wrote:

> *So you're saying if I am hurt over something, it means I have a desire that is surfacing and an idol in the heart, right? But isn't feeling hurt an emotion that is normal? Didn't God give us emotions? Do I turn every hurt and disappointment in on myself, saying, "Oh, I have idols. I am selfish, I am in sin, etc.?"*
>
> *Every time I feel hurt, I should feel guilty; every time I have a need or want I should feel guilty; I should think I really am not worthy of anything, is that it? I guess I should just forget all about my wants/needs/desires/likes/dislikes . . . and not even feel, think, or react to anything.*
>
> *I do see idols and I give them to God, but they keep popping back up. I want to be right with God—*

I don't like this struggle—but I am not convinced that giving up everything that is important to me is really right, or the answer, or even what God wants. Why would He want me to be unhappy?

At first, you might feel empathy for Maura. She is trying so hard and she is hurting. However, you can hear the idolatry in her frustration, her self-pity and confusion, and her efforts to control. You can also hear a hint of works-based sanctification.

Maura's idols "keep popping up" because—by her own confession—she's never really asked God to remove them. They're still there and they're still causing destruction. She testifies to her dependency on them, but sees giving them up as an act of martyrdom, rather than an act of worship correction.

Her lack of confidence in trusting God is summarized by her last sentence: *"I'm not convinced that giving up everything that is important to me is really right, or the answer, or even what God wants."* Maura wants to please God—as long as she can keep trying to please herself.

Her sarcastic and somewhat insincere offer to *"just forget about all my wants/needs/desires/likes/dislikes . . . and not even feel, think, or react to anything,"* sounds more like a petulant child than someone seeking to please God. It's if she were saying, "You don't want me to have any desires, God? Fine. I won't have any. *Now* am I holy enough to please You?" A few days later, she wrote:

Why do I always have to try to be pleasing to God, when everyone else gets to do whatever they want? Sometimes I wonder if God even loves me at all. If He did, He would not make this so hard.

I love that email, because it so perfectly expresses all of our hearts when we are struggling with God over our desires:

God says: “Be holy.”
We say: “I’d rather be happy.”

As we continued to correspond, Maura seemed stuck above the one-way mirror on the Self-pleasing side of the Idols Chart—seeing only a reflection of her pain, the hurtful things others were doing, and her efforts to be godly. The sorrow she most often expressed was not humble and godly sorrow because of sin, but worldly sorrow because of her inability to control others. She wanted God to change *other* people most of all.

You might think I’m being hard on Maura, but I care for her very much and want her to experience the freedom and joy of God in *every* aspect of her life. Recently, Maura has acknowledged she is not living as a child of God. She is confident He gave her a new heart when she accepted Christ, but nonetheless admits she has been using her new heart like the old one, trying to gain control and refusing to submit to Him. The day Maura truly seeks the Lord with *all* her heart, she will find Him (Jeremiah 29:13). Then, her emails will sound more like this:

> *All this time I have been focused on how I was hurting, what I wanted, and how other people were interfering in my ability to have what I desired. I never realized that clinging to that desire was a form of worship. I was so worried about everyone else*

sinning against me and so proud that I wasn't sinning against them in return, that I never realized I was in the greater sin—sin against God Himself, by worshipping what I desired. May He purify my heart, renew a right and steadfast spirit in me, and restore to me the joy of salvation. Amen.

☙ ❧

A rich young ruler approached Jesus and asked, "Good teacher, what must I do to get (inherit) eternal life?" Having power and authority, he was accustomed to confidently pursuing what he wanted and showed not a hint of self-consciousness or hesitation in approaching the man he considered a great teacher (Matthew 19:16-26, Mark 10:17-31, Luke 18:18-27

Jesus could have responded by answering the man's question directly, saying, "Believe in Me and you will have eternal life (John 14:1)"—but to a man of power and wealth, this would have seemed an unsatisfactory answer. If all that was required for eternal life was faith, *all* his power and money were of no advantage.

Jesus also could have said, "I am the way, the truth and the life. Believe in Me and you will be saved (John 14:6)." However, in that day being saved generally meant being delivered from dangerous circumstances or physical oppression, or made and kept safe (John 5:34 AMP).

"Okay, fine," the man might have responded, "but I don't need to be *saved.* What I want to know is how to gain eternal life."

So, Jesus told the man there was *nothing* he could do to inherit eternal life. *"No one is good except God alone,"* He said.

To us, that may seem like a curious interjection in the middle of the conversation, but Jesus knew that in order for the rich young ruler to understand and accept the answer to his question, he had to first understand that he *couldn't* be good. The Law, with which the man would have been familiar, was given to reveal the need for salvation (Romans 3:19-20).

Jesus' statement, "No one is good except God alone," was the conclusion of the Law; but the rich young ruler, secure in his self-sufficiency and trusting in his wealth, didn't recognize that. So, Jesus patiently began at the beginning, leading him step-by-step to the truth. *"If you want to enter eternal life, keep the commandments."*

Had the rich ruler been the slightest bit aware of his own unrighteousness, he might have responded, "I've tried, but I am not able!" He could have confessed exactly what Jesus had said a moment earlier: "But no one is good except God alone!" He could even have exclaimed what the disciples were to say later: "But Lord, who then can inherit eternal life?" Instead, without hesitation he asked, "Which commandments?"

It was such a simple question, but it revealed so much. Clearly, he did not take seriously God's requirement that obeying the Law required obeying the *whole Law* perfectly. He was looking for a shortcut, not a Savior.

Jesus listed six of God's commands—specifically, those most easily observed by others. *"You shall not murder, commit adultery, steal, or lie. You must honor your father and mother, and love your neighbor."*

The ruler could have admitted, "I tried, but was not able," or again, he could have simply repeated Jesus' earlier statement: "But no one is good except God alone." Instead, without missing a beat, he eagerly proclaimed himself to be good, saying, "All of these I have kept since I was a boy. What do I still lack?"

Imagine the foolishness of declaring his innocence in the presence of everyone who had known him since birth—and the audacity of doing so just after Jesus had said *no one* was good. It was so human and so sad, so utterly ridiculous, yet so much like each of us.

There was little reason for Jesus to list the commandments having to do with worship and obedience of the heart. A man who so easily claimed to keep the observable commands would of course say he had perfectly observed the private ones as well. *Jesus looked at the man with love.*

Here was a man who had deceitfully proclaimed his own righteousness, a man about whom nothing said, "I love the Lord, my God." Yet, Jesus looked on him with love—not for who the ruler was, what he had done, or what he would do—but because Jesus knew He was about to bring the man to a spiritual crisis. What He said next was with love, not condemnation; but it would shake the ruler to the core of his being and reveal the truth condition his heart. Jesus was about to give the man the answer to his question of how to gain eternal life.

"If you want to be perfect . . ." Jesus began.

We can almost picture the man leaning forward, certain he had thus far proven his righteousness. His head nodding in anticipation and the words, "I have done that, too!" were surely already formed on his lips.

"If you want to be perfect . . . there's one thing you lack. Go sell your possessions and give to the poor, and you will have treasure in heaven. Then, come follow me." With that challenge, Jesus threw open the door to the man's heart, lit the darkness with His glory, and exposed the man's trust in wealth and power. He essentially said, "Rid yourself of confidence in these things and put your trust in Me."

The man slammed the door to his heart shut, fearing the challenge to trust in God alone. Then he went away sad, because he had great wealth.

Jesus looked at His disciples and said, *"Truly I tell you, it is hard for someone who is rich to enter the kingdom of heaven."* It wasn't a comment about the wealthy being unable to be saved; but the disciples must have thought so, for they were stunned.

"Who then can be saved?" they asked.

If Jesus had answered, "Only the poor and powerless," we would have seen this as a lesson in comparative spirituality between the wealthy and the impoverished. What He said instead was a lesson in trust.

No one can follow Christ wholeheartedly, or trust in God completely, as long as they are holding onto whatever they feel they must have for security, peace, or happiness. Letting go of those idols of the heart is utterly contrary to human nature; but Jesus reassures the disciples—and us: *"With man this is impossible, but with God all things are possible" (Matthew 19:26).*

ᏣᏰ ᏈᏜ

Some idols are easy to see, confess, and toss off the throne of our heart. Others require God's help, though we may leave bloody fingernail trails down their sides as we reluctantly see them go. Then, there are those idols or desires we have made so crucial to our happiness, and so much a part of our identity or self-protection, that just the *thought* of relinquishing them fills us with dread.

The prospect of letting go of the desire that seems most necessary for our happiness feels like not just allowing, but inviting, the most awful thing we can imagine into our lives—or at the very least, preventing what is good. We agonize over why God would require such a thing from us, for it is impossible in our natural state (Jeremiah 29:11). We can only ask Him to remove that desire, which is like handing a surgeon a knife and asking him to heart surgery on our heart . . . without anesthesia. It is a death of Self, made possible only by faith in Jesus Christ, through the Spirit of God residing within us (1 Corinthians 1:30, 2:12). Yet, the life that follows from that death is sweet.

ᏣᏰ ᏈᏜ

Not long after I began teaching on idols of the heart, my husband accepted a job that took him to Iraq as a contractor, for sixteen weeks at a time. Halfway through the first rotation, I noticed his endearments began to seem forced and he had less and less to say in our phone calls and emails. He was faithfully going through the motions, but his heart and attention were obviously somewhere else. When I asked him about the change, nothing in his reassurances gave me comfort.

Asking God to reveal whatever was hidden and disclose whatever was concealed (Luke 8:17), I found evidence my husband's affection and attention were turned toward a co-worker. A downcast face and tormenting spirit became my constant companions, bringing me to my knees again and again, as I wrinkled the pages of Job and Psalms with my tears.

Friends said it was a ploy of Satan to hurt my ministry, but I knew otherwise. Ever since my late teens, when my dad abandoned my mom for another woman, I had determined no man would ever betray me. The desire for a faithful husband had long been one of the biggest idols of my heart and the filter through which I weighed nearly every decision in my life, in some form. There was no way God was going to let me teach on idols of the heart, without addressing my own.

Realizing that, however, did not make things easier. God was requiring me to relinquish all the trust I had put in the desire for my husband faithfulness. I was terrified doing so would result in losing him—a fate I could not bear to imagine. I felt like I was standing at the edge of a monstrously dark and deadly swamp, with God asking me to step into it as a condition for pleasing Him. As far as I was concerned, He might as well have been asking me to submit myself to being tortured alive.

"I want to, God, but I can't," I cried. As soon as I said those words, however, I knew it was a lie. I *could* step forward in faith. I just wasn't willing to do so, for fear of the death sure to follow. Then, I remembered Jesus had gone through death into life. He knew the way and would carry me.

At that moment, it seemed as if Jesus were standing beside me with His arms open wide, telling me to fall into Him. Closing my eyes, I mentally wrapped my arms around His neck, pulled my legs up, hid my face in His shoulder, and braced for the darkness and terror I knew would come next.

Instead, there was only silence—like the silence after a midnight snow—and peace. The raging storm that had occupied my spirit for so many months was gone. "What happened to the hell I thought I had to go into?" I asked.

"Your faith has made you whole" (Mark 5:34), He said.

Nothing in my circumstances had changed, but my fears and anxieties were completely stilled (Mark 4:35-41). It was putting my trust in a powerless idol to protect me that had been my torment, not God. Clinging to Christ, I had let that idol go, and it had crashed in pieces on the floor.

Three days later, the situation at my husband's work changed in such a way that every temptation for him was removed—confirmation to me that God had arranged or at least allowed it all in order to purify my heart. No doubt He had used it to challenge and grow my husband as well, but I was most grateful for what He had done in me.

The amount of brokenness and time it took for me to surrender to God only proved how deeply rooted that particular idol had been. I thought God had been asking so much, but He had only been asking me to worship Him alone. He didn't say He would deny me my desires or that I couldn't have them—only that I couldn't put my trust in them. How ironic it was that I had been willing to trust God with my *eternal* future, yet utterly terrified to trust Him with my tomorrow.

7. The Challenge of Trust

If anyone would come after me, let him deny himself and take up his cross daily and follow me (Luke 9:23).

Over the next eight months, painful memories and heartaches occasionally resurfaced, but never with the same intensity as before. Still, I was unable to put my husband's emotional adultery behind me, even though if only for lack of opportunity there had been no physical adultery.

I needed him to realize how much he had hurt me, and show enough sorrow and regret that I would feel safely confident he would never do it again. In a way, I wanted him to pay a price for his sin, in order to forgive him. He soon grew weary of my efforts to accomplish that goal.

I will never forget the day I called him from a pastor's house in South Africa, where I was speaking. Everything was going beautifully with my trip, but that morning something had sparked another wave of memories and resentment in my heart. I knew his former co-worker was still trying to communicate with him; and though he wasn't responding, it was a regular reminder of what had happened. I felt increasingly distant.

"What's wrong?" he asked, when we spoke.

"Nothing," I lied, with a cool tone.

He pressed until I admitted my dissatisfaction.

"That *still?*" he asked in angry exasperation. Then he added, "I'm done. I'm just done!"

Those kinds of phrases were never said in our marriage, and normally would have turned me into a teary mess; but God's peace sustained me—despite the sin stirring in my heart.

Stating the facts simply and firmly, I said: "No! I clung to you and prayed for you when you were slipping away. I am slipping away right now, in a different way, and you need cling to me and pray for me." Those words still surprise me, today.

What happened next could only have been of God. My husband asked, "Right now?" I said, "Yes," and he prayed the most sincere, loving, and healing prayer I could ever have imagined. My heart was softened; and from that day forward, the painful memories were quieted.

Not long after that, God helped me understand I had replaced the former idol of having a faithful husband with a new idol of wanting my husband to know how much he had hurt me. He also showed me that my husband would *never know* the depth of my pain until the Last Day, when all was revealed. Then, it wouldn't matter anymore; because on that day, everything I had done and all the hurt I had caused others would also be revealed—and we both would be made clean in Christ.

> *Do not despise the Lord's discipline or be weary of His reproof, for the Lord reproves whom He loves, as a father the child in whom he delights (from Proverbs 3:11-12).*

Relinquishing the idol of wanting my husband to know how much pain I had endured, I had God's peace. So much so, that even when I looked for the former hurt, I could no longer find it. Forgiveness came easy then, and somewhere along the way, God also gave me forgiveness for my dad.

7. The Challenge of Trust

As far as the east is from the west, so far does He remove our transgressions from us (Psalm 103:12).

My growing understanding of idolatry was soon put to the test, when my husband received an offer to work in Australia. This time, he was given the option of having me accompany him—a decision he left up to me. The chance to live in Australia was exciting, and I was delighted to have the opportunity to be together again.

Relocating halfway across the world, however, was filled with complications. First, I feared it would break my elderly parents' heart. They could also become ill or even pass away while I was gone. Second, my relationship with my adult son—which had been damaged when I moved away in his teens—was just starting to heal after a decade of prayer. I feared leaving would undo the small steps of progress we had made.

Yet when I thought of *not* going, I feared what might happen to my marriage. I appreciated all I had learned from the previous experience, but I certainly had no desire to repeat it.

No matter which decision I considered—to stay or to go—there was a potentially idolatrous desire corrupting that decision. I wanted my decision to be made solely on the basis of seeking to please God. Not knowing what else to do, I laid my conflicting desires before God, confessed my wrong worship, and recalled His Word as the only thing I knew for sure:

Lord, I desire to be with my husband and have a good marriage, and I desire to have a good relationship with my son and his family-to-be. I don't want to hurt my parents and I don't want to miss their last years. These seem like good desires, but I don't want them to be idols in my life. I relinquish all my desires to You, as an offering. Your Word says I am one with my husband and he is my head, so I will go with him, trusting everything else to You. I go joyfully, without fear or looking back, seeking only to please You in all I do and welcoming whatever You desire to do in me. In Jesus' name, amen.

So, I packed up the house and moved to Australia to join my husband, leaving my parents' health and the relationship with my son in God's hands. There were many joys and challenges while we were in Australia, but each one provided another opportunity to grow in learning what it meant to seek to please God above all else.

Meanwhile, back home God sustained my parents' health. My son married the woman he had been dating and they invited me to stay with them whenever I was in town. As a result, I grew closer to them than if I had not moved away.

I am certain had I made the decision to move, out of fear of what would happen to my marriage if I didn't; or decided *not* to move, out of fears regarding my son and parents, those decisions would *not* have been blessed at all. Conversely, I am just as certain had I decided *not to move*, out of a desire to please God (to honor my parents, for example), God would have blessed *that* decision as much as He blessed my going.

What I did, in other words, was not as important as my motivation for doing it.

> *The one who eats, eats in honor of the Lord, since he gives thanks to God, while the one who abstains, abstains in honor of the Lord and gives thanks to God . . . (Romans 14:6).*

We moved back home to the U.S., just as my son's first child was born. I had never considered—much less wanted—to take on the role of caring for a grandchild, but I suddenly couldn't imagine anything else. Having not been a believer when I raised my son, it has been one of my greatest joys to help raise my granddaughter in the wisdom of the Lord. For the time being, her parents have allowed me to homeschool her, providing *limitless* opportunities to seek to please God daily. I'm amazed how God not only satisfied the desires I *knew* I had in my heart, but even desires I hadn't known I had.

> *And she was amazed at the greatness of God (from Luke 9:43 NIV).*

ƐƆƆƷ

When God told Abraham to sacrifice his beloved son, Abraham set out to do so without so much as a whimper of "Why, God?" (Genesis 22). Who of us would have done such a thing? In our more honest moments, we might even admit to being as discomforted by God's command to Abraham, as by Abraham's willingness to obey. Yet, it is the offensiveness of that command that makes it so significant as a foreshadowing of an even greater offense: God's sacrifice of His own beloved and perfect Son.

Likewise, God's gracious and wondrous setting-free of Isaac, by the provision of a substitute ram, foreshadowed the even greater setting-free of everyone who trusts in God's raising-up of His Son from death to life (Romans 14:9). The ram lived and died. Jesus died and lives—so that *all* who call on His name may have new life in Him (Romans 10:13).

If you believe in Jesus' resurrection, you no longer live for yourself, but for Him (2 Corinthians 5:15). You rejoice that He gave Himself for you, so that you might be set free from the power of sin and zealously desire to do good (Titus 2:11-14). Buried with Christ by baptism into death, you have been raised from death to new life, by the glory of the Father (Romans 6:4).

> *If anyone would come after me, let him deny himself and take up his cross and follow me. For whoever would save his life will lose it, but whoever loses his life for my sake will find it (Matthew 16:24-25).*

ଓ ଛଓ ଛ

UPDATE 2018:Ten years have passed since the initial incident told in this chapter, and five years since we returned home. My husband and I are celebrating twenty years of marriage, continuing to joyfully grow in love and godliness.

Chapter 7 ~ Homework

1. Why is the best time to look for idols when you are angry, sad, or anxious? Why is it also the most difficult time? Does that mean you don't have idols of the heart at other times?

2. Can you recall a situation in which you were scared to relinquish a desire because you worried it then might never come to pass; or scared to relinquish a fear, because you were anxious it might permit what you fear to come to pass? What happened?

Chapter 7 - Prayer

Lord God,

I thank You, O God, and give You praise, for You are my strength and my shield. My heart trusts in You and You alone, for You are good and Your love endures forever. My heart rejoices in You and I praise Your Name, for Your kingdom cannot be shaken. I give You my gratitude, with reverence and awe; for You, O God, are a consuming fire (Psalm 103:9, 28:7, 69:30; Hebrews 12:28-29). You turn my wailing into dancing. You remove my sackcloth and clothe me with joy. My heart sings Your praises and will not be silent. Oh Lord, my God, I will praise You forever (Psalm 30). I thank You in the name of Jesus Christ, amen.

Journal

Write about how you have been trusting God in the situation you chose for this study. Has your understanding of trusting God changed at all? Are you comfortable with that change?

Section 2

Helping Others

Little children, keep yourselves from idols.
(1 John 5:21)

8. Suffering and Grief

Having a troubled spirit or downcast face does not necessarily mean a person is in idolatry. Although the Bible tells us all sin leads to suffering—a point Jesus confirmed when He said, "Go and sin no more, that nothing worse may happen to you" (John 5:14), and He affirmed when He said He healed as a demonstration of His authority on earth to forgive sins (Mark 2:10)—the Bible confirms not all suffering or sadness is caused by one's own sin.

For example, Jesus also said a particular man's suffering was *not because of sin,* but so that the works of God might be displayed" (John 9:1-3). He, Himself, wept over Jerusalem (Luke 19:41). The Holy Spirit grieved Israel's spiritual adultery (Isaiah 63:10). The prophets Isaiah, Jeremiah, and Nehemiah mourned and grieved the rebellion of God's people.

When God showed the prophet Daniel a vision for the future of His people, Daniel said, "My thoughts troubled and alarmed me much and my cheerfulness of countenance was changed in me" (Daniel 7:28 AMP). That may sound like the symptoms of idolatry, but it was an expression of godly grief.

We are not Jesus, the Holy Spirit, or the prophets; but as believers in Christ we should expect to suffer for the faith (John 15:21, Acts 9:16, 1 Peter 3:14) or for doing good (1 Peter 2:19).

Therefore, it is certainly possible to experience suffering that is not the direct result of our own sin.

Richard Wurmbrand, an evangelist who experienced years of torture and imprisonment for sharing the Gospel in a communist country, describes his experience of suffering for the Gospel (2 Timothy 1:8) and the supernatural comfort of Christ that accompanied that suffering[14]:

> *It was in prison that we found the hope of salvation for the Communists. It was there that, we developed a sense of responsibility toward them. We knew the communists were controlled by the devil and pitied them. It was in being tortured by them that we learned to love them.*
>
> *The soles of my feet were beaten to the bone, then beaten to the bone again the next day—the pain of which there are no words to describe. I saw other Christians with fifty pounds of chains on their feet, tortured with red-hot iron pokers, in whose throats spoonfuls of salt had been forced, being kept afterward without water, starving, whipped, suffering from cold—and yet still praying with fervor for the Communists. This is humanly inexplicable! It is the love of Christ, poured out in our hearts.*
>
> *In our darkest hours of torture, the Son of Man came to us, making the prison walls shine like diamonds and filling the cells with light. Somewhere, far away, were the torturers below us in the sphere of the body. But the spirit rejoiced in the Lord. We would not have given up this joy for kingly palaces.*

Few, if any, of us in the West have ever experienced such persecution; but believers in other parts of the world know it well. In some countries, every Christian family has a member who has been imprisoned, discriminated against, tortured, or murdered because of their faith.

I'm told not one of us knows how we will respond to such persecution or trials of faith, until the moment comes. However, we know that faith tested by the fires of suffering and found genuine is more precious than gold; that if we have suffered with the attitude of Christ, we are finished with sin; and that we should share in Christ's sufferings with rejoicing (1 Peter 1:7, 4:1, 13). We can only truly experience God when we draw near to Him, and nothing causes us to draw as near to Him as suffering.

> *Count it all joy . . . when you meet trials of various kinds, for you know that the testing of your faith produces steadfastness. And let steadfastness have its full effect, that you may be perfect and complete, lacking in nothing (James 1:2-4).*

Although not all suffering is caused by a person's own sin, it is not cruel or wrong to talk about idolatry with them. Even if that was not the cause of their suffering, it is often involved in their response to that suffering. There, it will magnify their pain, deepen their grief, and separate them from God's peace and comfort . . . just when they need it the most.

☙ ❧

Some years ago, I met three Christian women in a Muslim country who had started a weekly day camp program for their children and others in their church. Muslim neighbors had asked if their children could also attend the camp, and the women—knowing how sensitive the issue could be—agreed on the condition that the children's fathers approved. Consequently, several Muslim children attended, with some of their parents coming to enjoy the activities as well.

Soon, however, the local imams began broadcasting accusations that the women were trying to convert the Muslim children. People grew angry and the women were arrested. During the trial, mobs rioted in the streets, carrying coffins with the women's names on them and calling for their deaths. To the court's credit, the women's lives were spared; but they were sent to prison for several years—leaving behind husbands, young children, and businesses.

Their lives were wonderful examples of what it means to seek to please the Lord at all times. When I visited them in prison, it felt like I was visiting their homes on Christmas Day. They grieved being separated from their families, but they were filled with the joy of Lord, as God was worked in and through them to bring His light into such a dark place.

The following year, I was on my way to Kenya to visit some women in prison there, but a warden strike resulted in a cancellation of those plans. The same day, however, my host received permission for to visit refugee camps, where hundreds of thousands of Christians had been living since horrible post-election violence, six months earlier.

Walking among the rows of tents in the first camp, I heard story after story of lost homes and farms, neighbor turned against neighbor, and family members killed while trying to escape. Turning a corner, I saw a man sitting on an overturned bucket in front of his tent, quietly reading the Bible to a small group of people at his feet. It was a scene that stopped me in my tracks and seared itself into my memory. Instead of mourning the past, he was worshipping God. Instead of dwelling on the present, he was worshipping God. Instead of worrying about the future, he was worshipping God.

I determined if I ever found myself in a situation where my daily life was so completely upended that nothing of it remained, I would follow his example and not waste time in self-pity or despair, but make it my priority to worship God and share Him with others. Then I prayed I would begin to do that now.

In the sixth and largest camp, the overall atmosphere was much more hopeful and busy than in the others. Resident teachers had begun a school for the older children, younger children were playing happily among the tents, and many people had started small businesses with items brought by friends from outside the camp. When I commented on the obvious difference, I was told that a group of pastors and others met at four o'clock every morning to pray for the camp, and done so since the day it opened.

One of those pastors was so cheerful, I was surprised to learn he had gone back to his village to offer reconciliation, only to be sent back with an eye gouged out and a hand cut off. What surprised me even more was that I hadn't even noticed the missing eye and hand at first, so great was his joy in the Lord. How was it possible, I wondered, that a person could suffer so much and still be so happy?

That pastor asked me to speak to the people who had gathered, but I felt inadequate to the task. "Give them a word of encouragement," he urged. "They feel as though God has forgotten them."

I had only prepared a message on idolatry for the women I had planned to visit in prison—a word of conviction about sin, not one of comfort or encouragement for people who were suffering the sins of others. Silently, I prayed and ask God to tell me what He wanted me to say.

"You were given a message on idolatry," I felt the Holy Spirit say in my heart. *"That is why you were brought here and that is what you are to share."*

"That hardly seems appropriate for the circumstances," I protested. "Isn't there something else?"

Just then, a whirlwind of dust rose up from the ground, engulfing the large tent where we were gathered. The sides came loose and flapped so hard, the whole thing seemed ready to collapse. Plastic chairs tumbled past my feet, as I covered my eyes to protect against the wind and sand. Someone yelled, calling for help to steady an adjacent, smaller tent. Then, as suddenly as it had begun, the whirlwind stopped.

Coincidence or not, I wasn't going to take any chances. After everything was back in order, I took a deep breath, looked around at the faces of the suffering and heartbroken people who had assembled and began: "In every circumstance of life, really in every moment of life, you have a choice to seek to please yourself or seek to please God . . ."

When I was done, no one spoke or stirred, and I self-consciously thought how arrogant it was of me to talk about idols of the heart to people who were suffering so much. In a few days, I was going to board a plane and go back to my comfortable home. They no longer had homes to return to.

I was trying to figure out how to exit politely, when a man stood and said, "I never thought of wanting my land and cattle back as an idol, but I see it now." Others nodded in agreement. A woman on the other side of the group stood and said she realized she had been worshipping an idolatrous desire for revenge.

Several others gave testimonies of what God was showing them, concluding with prayers and surprise at the way He was filling their hearts with peace. One man wrote a poem on a scrap of paper and shared it with the group, expressing the change God was working in his heart that day. They were still grieving, but something was different. Their grief was no longer darkened by resentment, rage, or fear. They had the comfort and peace of God.

Afterwards, I sat privately with a woman who had run away to safety with their children, while her husband had been thrown in a well to die. Her nights were haunted by nightmares of leaving him behind, and her days were filled with regret and the pain. If not for her children, she said, she wished she had stayed and died with her husband.

I wept with her over her loss. Then, I gently suggested the possibility that her guilt could be a type of sacrifice, and the nightmares a type of offering, to an idol of wanting to make sense of why such a thing could have happened and protect against it happening in the future to her or her children. That sounds a little odd to me now, but it was what I felt the Holy Spirit put on my heart to say.

She lifted her head and looked at me with surprise, saying my words described exactly what she felt. She asked me to pray with her as she confessed her heart and prayed God would remove whatever idols might be found there. When she opened her eyes, her face was filled with God's peace.

Any remaining worry I had of offending people who were hurting, by helping them examine their hearts for idolatry, was wiped away that day, for I had seen clearly that the God who gives life is the God who gives comfort and peace.

> *[He comforts] all who mourn; giving them a beautiful headdress instead of ashes, the oil of gladness instead of mourning, the garment of praise instead of a faint spirit; that they may be called oaks of righteousness, the planting of the Lord, that He may be glorified (Isaiah 61:2-3).*

☙ ❧

Understanding how idols of the heart separate us from God's peace and comfort is particularly important for those suffering the death of a loved one, as Jessica testifies:

Jessica's Testimony

Jessica joined our small group on idols of the heart a year after her six-year-old daughter died, but we didn't know of her loss until the last week of the class. We were surprised to learn how much she had gone through over the past six years.

"When I first started coming to this study," she said, "I thought I was dealing with my daughter's death pretty well, but I was still struggling. Now, God has shown me an idol of my heart I would never have thought of as an idol before, but one that has been keeping me from experiencing His full peace."

This is her story:

> *My little girl, Teagan, fell into a coma from an infection when she was just eleven months old and suffered severe brain damage. Suddenly the sweet baby I had known could not see, make noise, or move. I didn't understand why God would give me a gift of a healthy little girl, just to take her away.*
>
> *We prayed constantly for healing, and ten months after the coma, she suddenly began to see, smile, sit up, and even giggle again. We were overjoyed and praised God, although we still hoped for a full recovery.*
>
> *"If only she could walk," I thought, "I would be happy." I even took for granted the gift of sitting up and complained to God that it wasn't enough. "But God, she needs to walk!" I prayed.*
>
> *After two years of being able to sit up and interact with us a bit, Teagan lost all she had gained and once again became unable to move hardly at all I was so angry with God. "But I am a Christian!" I cried. "I have had my share of suffering already in this world. My daughter has suffered enough. Please don't take away what little You have given her."*

I continued to beg God to heal our sweet girl. "I know You can heal her! Why won't You?" I asked. I didn't know it then, but I was praying Control for Success prayers, even bargaining with God, saying, "If You heal her I will tell everyone it was You."

After two more years, we decided it was time to let her go, and we were finally able to take her out on some outings to the beach and the river—things we had been unable to do before, when we were protecting her health. She died of pneumonia on my birthday; but her face was radiant with the light of God, and it was a peaceful experience.

After they took her away, however, I broke down. Doubt crept in: "What had I done? I had stopped fighting to keep my baby alive! Had I let her down?" I was stricken with grief and didn't know what to do. The pain filled every ounce of my being. How could I be thankful for the suffering God had let my daughter endure? How could I be thankful for the pain I was feeling? I wasn't sure how to trust a God who had caused her—and me—so much pain.

Understanding idols of the heart helped me see that although I had given my daughter back to God—which I had thought was submitting to Him on the highest level—I was still struggling with Him about her life of suffering. I had made an idol of trying to make sense of it all, thinking I was leading a godly life, but still trying to please myself by clinging to the need to have an answer.

> *I realized my whole Christian life had been telling God what I wanted Him to do, as if He owed me. I confessed idols of wishing things had been different, wishing our daughter hadn't suffered and died, wishing our family hadn't suffered, wanting to know why God allowed it, and wanting her back.*
>
> *But I couldn't let go of those idols, no matter how much I tried, because I was terrified. The pain I was holding on to was the last piece of my daughter I had on this earth. It connected me to her, and I just couldn't allow God to take that away, too.*
>
> *When you said that submitting to God is like dying to ourselves, I realized I had been trying to get rid of those idols on my own. I asked God to remove them for me, and the heavy burden was lifted off my chest. For the first time, I truly felt the peace of God that passes all understanding.*

A year later she wrote again, adding to her testimony of God's enduring peace:

> *God's peace is still with me, and my faith makes sense to me in ways it never did before. I think recognizing grief as an idol of the heart is one of the hardest things to understand, because it is masked with pain that seems pure, but is really eating you up. God is not in that. I had thought it would dishonor my daughter if I gave up my grief, because I felt closer to her when I was at my lowest. How the devil was deceiving me! My focus is now on resting in God's assurance and peace.*

ଓ ଓ

Tracey's Testimony

I first met Tracey when my husband and I began attending the church where her husband, Graham, was the pastor. Shortly after we joined the church, Graham was diagnosed with cancer. Here is Tracey's testimony:

> *When we first learned of Graham's diagnosis we were devastated. We knew it would be easy to give ourselves over to fear and idolatry, so we prayed we would not be disempowered by our despair, but empowered to bring God glory through it all. We sought out every possible treatment, but in pursuing them, we had peace that God was sovereign and knew that no matter what happened, we would still seek to serve and please Him every step along the way.*
>
> *Daily, we read through Psalms and Proverbs together, and I was struck afresh with the idea of seeking first God's kingdom and His righteousness. So often I prayed for everything else first, like the kids doing well, etc.—and it suddenly grieved me. God knows everything, even what I fear for my children and my husband. Yet I forget. Somehow I think, "If I don't pray, maybe nothing will happen!"*
>
> *Sometimes, I wondered whether being strong and godly meant holding in my feelings—or having*

the courage to be real and vulnerable, without fear or embarrassment.

When Graham died, I was surprised by all the theological opinions people offered about why he got cancer, and I wondered how much heartache a person could endure, or if the pain would ever cease.

A few months later, one of my closest friends committed suicide, and my head was spinning with the dichotomy that she would take her own life, when my husband had been fighting so hard for his.

Every time I felt my heart slipping into idolatrous kinds of thoughts and fears, I went to God again in prayer and He gave me peace. I never blamed God and my grief never became destructive. Instead, it caused me to rely even more on Him and His Word for Truth, taking comfort in knowing He had seen His own son suffer and die.

Since then, I have pursued God anew, and live with a joy in the Lord even greater than before. How is that even possible? God is more powerful than I could have ever imagined. He has comforted me and given me peace, blessed me and freed me from the worries of this world. There is nothing, nothing I could add. In Him I am set free.

I posted Tracey's testimony on my website, with her permission, and one of the members of the church wrote a comment. Kate confessed she had judged Graham and Tracey, when she heard of Graham's diagnosis and death, and was deeply moved to repentance by Tracey's words. She wrote:

With a judgmental heart, I could not understand why Graham was ill. You looked like the perfect Christian family, and perfect Christian families are not supposed to suffer. So, I thought, "They can't be as good as they seem. Why would God punish them?" As much as I knew it was a terribly Pharisaic posture, it was only today, in reading your story, that God opened my eyes to see the sin in my own heart. I want to ask your forgiveness. Your testimony has not only convicted me of my sin, but encouraged and inspired me to keep trusting in God.

The judgment Kate admitted to feeling was something we all tend to do, when we see or hear of someone in suffering. If that person has values contrary to ours, we tell ourselves they are suffering God's punishment of sin. If their values are similar to ours, we assure them they have done nothing wrong and God isn't punishing them. Then we go home and wonder what they *must* have done wrong that we have not, in an effort to reassure ourselves of our own relative safety. Even when we are the ones suffering, we are more likely to question God's righteousness, than our own.

This human tendency to self-righteousness was the one thing Jesus addressed in the only instruction He gave His disciples about how to think on the causes of suffering. News had arrived that a group of people had been brutally murdered, and Jesus asked the disciples, "Do you think these Galileans were worse sinners than all the others because they suffered this way? I tell you, no!" (Luke 13:1-3).

Then He referred to another tragedy. "Or those eighteen who died when the tower in Siloam fell on them—do you think they were more guilty than all the others living in Jerusalem? I tell you, no!" (vv. 4-5). Jesus never said those who suffered were innocent. Nor did He say their suffering was the consequence of sin. In fact, He didn't talk about the reason or cause for their suffering, at all. He simply warned the disciples that unless they repented, they would likewise perish.

The message to us could not be any clearer. We are not to judge those in suffering as either righteous or sinful. Nor are we to imagine ourselves more righteous if we are not suffering the same. We are only to allow the suffering of others to remind us of our own inclination to sin, and repent.

☙ ❧

Suffering rips apart the connections we have to everyday life and strips away the illusion of control over our lives. In so doing, it provides an opportunity to experience surrendering to God at the deepest level of our souls—drawing closer to Him in a way so holy and sacred, it changes us forever. As David Powlison, in writing about his experience with cancer, said, "Suffering really is meant to wean you from sin and strengthen your faith."[15]

I find that thought encouraging. How much better it is to submit ourselves to God's refining hand, than waste even a moment claiming ourselves righteous victims. Personally, I would rather consider my suffering to be the consequence of my own sin and God's desire to conform me to the image of Christ

(Romans 8:29), than Satan trying to "take me down" or general evil that randomly strikes without warning or cause. At least I can do something about my own sin.

> *If we confess our sins, he is faithful and just to forgive us our sins and to cleanse us from all unrighteousness (1 John 1:9).*

ଓ ଡଓ ଡ

Chapter 8 - Homework

1. Have you experienced a diagnosis, tragedy, death, betrayal, or other suffering that has caused great grief? How has that experience impacted your faith?

2. Does relinquishing an idol (or asking God to remove it from the heart) mean you should not or cannot grieve? Give an example.

3. In what way might idolatrous grief look/feel different than non-idolatrous grief in a given situation?

Chapter 8 - Prayer

Lord God,

Hear my prayer, and do not hide Your face from me in the day of my distress. My days pass away like smoke, and my bones burn like a furnace; my heart is struck down like grass and has withered. I forget to eat my bread (Psalm 102:1-4). Shine Your light on me, oh Lord, and strengthen me. May I not be shaken, nor fear bad news; but have a heart that is secure and steadfast, trusting in You, Oh Lord (from Psalm 112:1-7). Even in my grieving, may I rest surely in Your faithfulness, knowing You will comfort me and give me peace. In the name of Jesus Christ, amen.

Journal

In your journal, or inside the back cover, draw an Idols Chart for a grief you have experienced—or use one of the testimonies in this chapter. Explain and show how James 1:15 applies, even in grief.

9. Models of Response

There are seven models or ways of responding to the trials and heartaches of life. The first six are very common and familiar. They are the surgical response, the chemical response, the behavioral response, the emotional response, the self-esteem response, and the spiritual response. The seventh is far less common and generally only turned to as a last resort, if at all. It is called the biblical response, because it applies biblical truth about worshipping God to life's problems.

The **surgical response** focuses on trying to separate from, change, or eliminate the perceived *cause* of difficulty or unhappiness. Removing oneself from a situation is the simplest example. Often utilizing the services of a professional, this model of response may include filing for bankruptcy, getting a divorce, repairing or replacing something broken, quitting an unpleasant job, taking medication to eliminate bacteria, or surgically removing a tumorous growth. Carried to the extreme, it might include murder or suicide. In any event, the hurting person is considered a victim of their circumstances.

The **chemical response** also views the individual as a victim, but focuses primarily on trying to reduce or eliminate the sensations or *symptoms* of a problem. Pain-relievers, endorphin-stimulating activities, chemical or food stimulants, and anti-depressants would all fall into this model of response. Whereas the surgical response has a specific time frame within which to achieve a defined resolution or cure, the chemical response may continue indefinitely. Incorrectly applied, this response treats all problems as though they were a physical condition, even when there is no cellular cause that can be identified by microscopic examination or quantifiable test. The collection of symptoms is then given a name, called a disease, and referred to as the cause of the very symptoms it describes.

The **behavioral response** focuses on changing a person's *behavior*. Examples might include identifying negative behaviors, practicing more desirable behaviors, learning to communicate effectively, implementing rewards to encourage good behavior, or establishing hindrances to discourage undesirable behavior. This model could also include taking action based on a resolution, such as "to get a job" or "to keep a house more orderly." Here, the unhappy person is viewed less as a victim of circumstances and more as a participant who needs instruction in more effective behavior. Incorrectly applied, this response becomes legalistic and controlling.

The **emotional response** focuses on modifying a person's *emotional or mental* responses to his or her circumstances. Self-analysis, psychological counseling, various self-help practices, and some forms of meditation would be included here, as well as identification of emotional triggers. Like the behavioral response, the emotional response views the unhappy person as having the power to affect his or her level of unhappiness by applying certain skills or knowledge. Even when this model of response includes changed behavior, however, the primary emphasis is on accomplishing that change through the understanding or management of underlying emotions. Carried to the extreme, the emotional response results in a lifestyle of enslavement to self-examination and mental preoccupation with "finding answers."

The **self-esteem response** involves responding to unhappiness by *redirecting* or diverting attention away from the perceived cause of unhappiness toward something that restores his or her sense of well-being. Examples could include going shopping in response to stress, making a significant lifestyle change in response to a painful event or life stage, or creating a "bucket list" of things to do in response to a terminal diagnosis. Misapplied, this model of response may or may not lead to behavioral sin, but could divert attention away from whatever God is trying to do in the heart in the original situation. It's tempting to think if something makes us happy it must be God's plan for us, or if it makes us unhappy it isn't; but the truth may be just the opposite.

The **spiritual response** relies on prayer, scripture, or other spiritual resources—of any faith or philosophy—for *comfort, healing, and encouragement*. From a Christian perspective, when this model of response is accurately applied it includes reading God's Word, praying for oneself and others, reflecting on the Gospel, and praising God. Misapplied, the spiritual response model fails to consider wrong worship in addressing problems, becomes rule-bound or legalistic regarding sin and behavior, treats Bible verses like superstitious incantations, or misapplies concepts of spiritual warfare.

The **biblical response** begins with confidence that pleasing God is our greatest source of peace and joy; that no sin is justified by another person's sin or the circumstances at hand; and that no other person's sin can prevent us from seeking to please God. In this model of response, problems are not looked upon as things to be overcome, but as opportunities to grow in Christ-likeness—so that His name will be proclaimed throughout the earth (from Ezekiel 36, Jeremiah 10).

The biblical response is like the surgical response in that it provides a definitive solution, the chemical response in that it is continually applied, the emotional response in that it looks inward, the behavioral response in that it leads to changed behavior, the self-esteem response in that it provides a sense of well-being, and the spiritual response in that it is grounded in faith. However, the biblical response is unique in that—unlike all the other models of response—it neither focuses on changing the circumstances nor on attaining happiness. Those things often result, but the primary focus is on identifying where the heart is not aligned with God and turning it back to Him.

> *Therefore now, says the Lord, turn and keep on coming to Me with all your heart . . . rend your hearts (in repentance for sin) and not your garments (in unhappiness for what has happened) and return to the Lord, your God (from Joel 2:12-13 AMP).*

Following the example of Jesus, the biblical response doesn't dwell on past sin or "beat people over the head" with the Bible. It does, however, speak easily and forthrightly of sin as something common to all.

9. Models of Response

Who can say, "I have made my heart pure; I am clean from my sin?" (Proverbs 20:9).

Practical suggestions may be given for what godly responses might look like in a situation, or suggestions made for "trying on" certain behavior—but not without also addressing the heart. At best, godly behavior from a wrong heart is never effective, no matter how perfectly it is carried out. At worst, it is corrupted with self-righteousness or self-pity and becomes sin.

☙ ❧

Each of the six common models of response is useful when correctly applied to the right situation, but the biblical response is *always* useful in *every* situation. Since wrong worship separates a person from God's blessing, it would be foolish or negligent to not at least *consider* the possibility of it.

That doesn't mean other responses can't be also applied. A person struggling with a physical disease can guard against an idol of the desire for life or healing (biblical response), while seeking medical treatment (surgical, chemical response) and prayer (spiritual response). The victim of a horrific crime can guard against making an idol of the desire that the crime had not happened or not happen again, while testifying against the perpetrator (surgical response), seeking counseling (emotional response), adopting defensive protections (behavioral response), and remembering God's word for fear (spiritual response).

☙ ❧

Savannah is a strong believer in Christ who has struggled with depression for three decades. She has taken a number of different medications, under the care of her psychiatrist (chemical response), and implemented various vitamin supplements or dietary changes, with the advice of a nutritionist (also chemical response). She has undergone numerous medical tests to try to find an underlying physical cause of her depression (surgical response), but none has yet been found.

At the advice of friends, she has tried "setting aside time for herself" (self-esteem response), or playing little mind games to try to motivate herself to do things (behavioral response). With a psychologist, she has analyzed and addressed painful events in her past (emotional response). With a Christian counselor, she has looked at possible areas of judgment or unforgiveness in her life (emotional and spiritual responses combined).

She has repented of past sin, sought prayer, and studied who she was in Christ (spiritual response). She has even successfully completed a difficult, advanced degree program toward a career in counseling (self-esteem response). When we first met for lunch at her request to talk about idols of the heart and depression, her prayer sounded like this:

> *Lord, please help me. I can't bear it any longer. Where are You? Why don't You answer? Please just take away this depression. In Jesus' name, amen.*

As Savannah examined her heart, she began to recognize that the desire "to not have depression" had become the focus of her worship. All of her thoughts were preoccupied with trying to satisfy that desire, all of her happiness rested on it coming about, and all of her trust for the future depended on it.

Yet, she was terrified confessing and relinquishing that desire as an idol was like telling God she didn't care and effectively inviting the depression to worsen. When she saw those feelings had no basis in truth, she set them aside and confessed the idol. Then her prayers began to sound more like this:

> *Lord, give me wisdom and perseverance to have a heart that seeks to please You more than myself. May my eyes be firmly fixed on what You want me do in all circumstances. May I grow in faith as You show me how to serve You, whether in strength or in weakness. I would like for my depression to be cured or lifted, but I ask You to remove that hope as an idol of my heart. May I make it my highest priority, to desire to please You, even if my circumstances never change. In Jesus' name, amen.*

Savannah still has periods of depression from time to time and still takes medication, but she is no longer enslaved by that depression or preoccupied with trying to get rid of it. Instead, she has come to think of depression as something God has allowed in her life for a reason. She now thinks more about how to please Him in and through her seasons of depression, than about how to get Him to take them away.

Rather than look on events and situations as possible "triggers," she has become more observant of how those events or situations tempt her to slip into idolatry. She focuses less on external things over which she has no control, now, and more on the possible sin in her heart's response.

Savannah writes: "I love that I can testify to what God has done in my life, even while He is working in me. Although I still struggle at times, learning to examine my heart has made me less fearful of those times and more interested in what God is trying to show me through them. I have peace now and have grown so much in my faith.

"I now know I don't have to be perfect in order for Him to use me, because His power is made perfect in my weakness and imperfection (2 Corinthians 12:8-10). The women in my church even asked me to lead a Bible study on depression and sadness, because they have seen such a huge difference in me and felt I could understand what they were going through."

☙ ❧

Vickie is a pastor's wife who has also struggled with depression for decades. Like Savannah, she has been managing her depression through various means, but wanted to examine her heart biblically. Here is her testimony of that experience:

> *The Lord showed me I was striving with Him regarding my depression and that in doing so, I was focusing on myself. It was not depression that was keeping me from joy; it was my focus on that depression and my determination to overcome it.*
>
> *Avoiding suffering had become an idol of my heart. I had thought, "If I didn't have depression, I*

> *would be a better person" . . . wrong. I can't do anything to make myself more pleasing to God, because His loving me has nothing to do with what I do, but rather with who I am: a repentant sinner saved by grace, a daughter of the King, adopted, and a joint heir with Christ. Since confessing my idolatry, there have been no dark clouds, and I no longer strive in that way anymore.*

☙ ❧

For as long as Cheryl could remember, her mother had struggled with depression, and Cheryl vowed in childhood never to be like her mother in that respect. As the Director of Children's Ministry in a large church, however, she often had to deal with conflict and criticism among the staff, which was painful and difficult. She was determined to keep a cheerful and caring demeanor (behavioral response), concerned if people knew how much she was struggling, they might say she was depressed. She was even more concerned they might be right.

As is so true of idolatry, the more fearful Cheryl became of being depressed, the more she clung to the idol of "not being depressed." The more she clung to that idol, the more depressed she became. Her sister said she should quit her job and find another that was less stressful (surgical response) and her best friend suggested she see a psychiatrist; but she was opposed to the idea of medication (chemical response).

Eventually, Cheryl did visit a Christian psychologist, where she gained some insight into her relationship with her mother (emotional response) and learned the four rules of communication[16] from the book of Ephesians 4:25-32 (spiritual response). However, there was little change in her depression.

The fact that God didn't seem to hear her prayers made Cheryl think maybe she wasn't pleasing Him enough. She thought about her parents' sins and wondered if she was suffering "generational bondage," or being "attacked by the devil" (spiritual response) for her role in the church. So, she committed to reading her Bible more each morning (behavioral or spiritual response) and praying for longer periods.

The first time Cheryl heard about idols of the heart, she immediately recognized the desire to not be like her mother as an idolatrous desire that had dominated much of her life. "Why hasn't anyone told me about this before?" she asked, with surprise. "All this time, I've been focusing on having good outward behavior in order to please God, not even realizing my heart was all wrong."

She repented of her idolatry and felt God immediately began to lift her out of darkness, into a peace unlike anything she had known before. Over the next several weeks, she also found she was more comfortable sharing her fears and disappointments with her staff—who told her she seemed more compassionate, approachable, and "real."

No longer feeling threatened by potential conflict, she began to see the challenges of her job as an opportunity to help others learn how to resolve disagreements in ways that glorified God. The thing that surprised her the most, however, was that—for the first time ever—she truly felt forgiveness and tenderness toward her mother.

ꕥ

The diagram below shows which area of the Idols Chart each model of response addresses: physical circumstances, behavior, or emotions. The biblical response is below the line, because it focuses on what is being worshipped in the heart. That may seem like a side issue, but is actually very important.

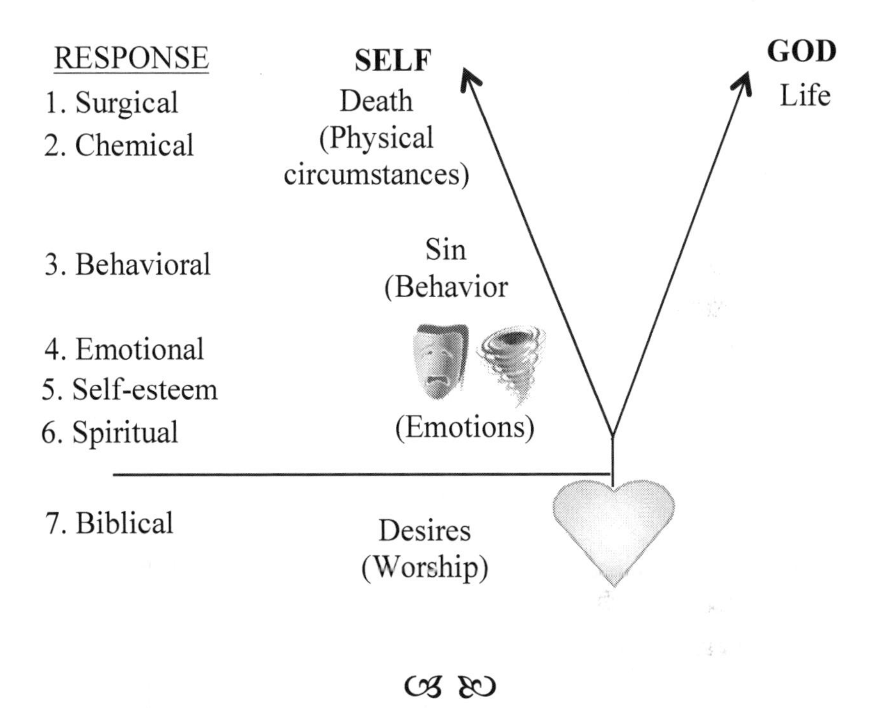

☙ ❧

Each model of response has its own vocabulary and worldview, so the model you tend to view problems through most will influence the way you think about, speak of, and respond to situations and problems.

For example, imagine you shared some confidences with Bob that your friend Kim had told you about herself. That night you laid awake, worried how upset Kim would be if she found out (human or false guilt from the fear of consequences).

You also feel guilty about having gossiped because you know it was against God's precepts (true guilt from dishonoring God), so you confess the matter to God. The next morning you decide to address it with Kim as well.

If you favor a surgical or chemical model of response, you tend to view the world and its problems through a "medical" lens, and your apology would sound something like the following. Notice the emphasis on physical images, a sense of victimhood, and the desire to fix things by taking action:

> *Kim, I don't know what* ***got into me*** *yesterday, but some things you told me* ***just slipped out*** *in my conversation with Bob.* ***I've been sick*** *about it ever since, and* ***tossed and turned*** *all night. What can I do* ***to fix things****?*

If you favor a behavioral or emotional model of response, you view the world and its problems through a "psychological" lens. Your apology would still have an element of victimhood, but less so than the medical worldview. Notice the emphasis on thinking and feeling:

> *Kim, I really* ***messed up****. Yesterday,* ***I wasn't thinking*** *and said some things about you to Bob* ***that I regret****. I* ***felt so guilty*** *about it all night, and I hope you won't be angry.* ***I'm so sorry****.*

If you favor a self-esteem model of response, you would emphasize each person's right to pursue happiness and feel good about themselves. Your response to the problem might be to skip the apology and just invite Kim to lunch, or shower her with approval and flattery to offset your transgression. If you did apologize, that apology would reflect your concern for maintaining happiness:

> *Kim, I accidentally told Bob what you said, but* ***don't worry****. He promised to keep it confidential. It's* ***all good****.* ***I love you*** *and would never intentionally do anything* ***to hurt you****, and I got you this* ***little gift****. If you're not doing anything this afternoon, please let me* ***make it up to you*** *by taking you to lunch.*

If you favor a spiritual model of response, you might justify your behavior as a response to Kim's sin or sincerely apologize from a convicted conscience:

> *Kim, I shared some things about you that I know you didn't want shared.* ***It was wrong*** *and I haven't* ***felt peaceful*** *ever since. I hope you will* ***forgive me. I'm so sorry.***

There's really nothing terribly wrong with any of those examples—except they could be spoken as easily by an atheist, agnostic, Buddhist, Jew, Muslim, or Hindu, as by a Christian. If you are a "new creation in Christ" (2 Corinthians 5:17), if you truly know you are "in this world but not of it" (John 17:16), shouldn't your words bear testimony to that truth?

The biblical model is a living testimony of your faith, because when you address problems using this response, you will speak in terms of personal sin, conviction, repentance, forgiveness, right worship, and faith:

> *Kim, yesterday I* ***sinned*** *against you by sharing things you had told me in confidence. That was* ***gossip*** *and the* ***Holy Spirit convicted*** *me that I* ***need*** *to ask your* ***forgiveness.*** *Because of what Christ has done for me, I want to live my life in a way that is* ***pleasing to God****, not conformed to the ways of this world. Will you forgive me?*

It doesn't matter whether Kim forgives you or not. It doesn't even matter whether she is a fellow believer. You are *testifying* about God by bearing witnessing to your confidence in His existence, the reality of the Holy Spirit in your life, the influence of the Gospel on your faith, and your desire to please God above all else.

> *Do not be conformed to this world, but be transformed by the renewal of your mind, that by testing you may discern what is the will of God, what is good and acceptable and perfect (Romans 12:2).*

☙ ❧

In the following story, try to identify which model of response each person favors, based on the suggestions or solutions they offer in response to Sandy's pain:

Sandy looked at the church's building committee meeting agenda in her hands. "I'm sorry," she said as she laid the papers aside. "I'm having a hard time concentrating on the new building tonight. In fact, I'm barely keeping it together."

"What's wrong?" asked Scott.

"My son just told my husband and me this past week that he is attracted to men."

"Wow," Scott said. "I had no idea."

"We had no idea either. We're in shock, really," Sandy added quietly. "We love him of course, but our hearts are broken. There are so many unanswered questions."

"Does he have a boyfriend?" asked Robin, the youngest and newest member of the committee.

"He says he does." Sandy struggled to go on. "He says they are planning to get married."

"How is the rest of your family taking it?" Scott asked.

"My husband is devastated. Our youngest son is heartbroken and won't even talk to him. Our daughter seems fine. She says, 'Mom, he's just the same guy as before'—and while I guess that's true, it doesn't really help. Our lives have been turned upside down." Sandy was fighting tears. "The idea of any man—much less my son—being sexually intimate with another man makes me nauseous. Marriage?" She shook her head and said, "I never dreamt I would have to deal with this."

Samuel said, "I'm so sorry. I can only imagine how hard this must be for you and your family. I'll be praying for you and for your son."

Robin asked, "If you love your son, don't you want him to be happy?"

"I don't think you understand, Robin," Sandy replied.

"I understand that God tells us to love others," Robin said pointedly, "and nothing is impossible with God."

"Maybe you could go together to see a counselor," Scott offered, "and figure out what's going on."

"He says he can't help the way he feels, that it's just the way he is," Sandy explained. "But I can't help the way I feel either. I've cried and prayed and asked God to change my heart if I'm wrong, but my feelings are as real for me as he says his are for him. I can't snap my fingers and make them go away."

"But if you give the impression you approve, it's like saying you don't take God's Word seriously," said Laurie. "I know it sounds harsh, but I read about a ministry leader in the same situation, who told her son he couldn't be part of their family anymore until he changed. He did change and they reconciled. I think you just need to take a firm stand on what is right and wrong."

"That's like him saying I can't be a part of his life unless I change, and I can't change. I can't sleep. I can't even think."

Kayla reached over and laid a slip of paper on Sandy's Bible. "Here's our doctor's contact. He gave me something last year for stress that helped a lot. Maybe you could give him a call."

"I think Sandy should love her son just as he is," Robin said. "I mean, isn't that what Jesus would do?"

"Jesus loved people who sinned, Robin, but not so they would stay the same," interjected Samuel. "He loved them so they would be changed. Sandy's son doesn't just want her love, he wants her approval for what she feels dishonors God."

"If I do what I think honors God's righteousness and His Word, by rejecting what I believe He calls sin," explained Sandy, "then I feel like I am dishonoring God by not being loving and accepting. If I honor God's command to love, by accepting my son, I violate my conscience about honoring God's righteousness."

"It's hard, Sandy," Haven said with compassion. "As Christians, we *are* called to honor God by loving others as Jesus loves us; but we are also called to respond by obedience to His Word. I honestly don't know what I would do in your shoes, but the fact you are grieving says a lot about how much you *do* love your son."

"Thank you for understanding. Yes, I do love him."

"Maybe you just need to have your son and his boyfriend over for dinner," Ethan offered. "Face your fears. It might not be as difficult as you think."

"I can't be a cheerful and welcoming hostess when I'm dying inside," Sandy said. "How am I supposed to pretend everything is okay, when it isn't?"

Nell was visibly upset. "I've known your son since junior high. How can he call himself a Christian? Doesn't he even care what God thinks?"

"I asked him the same thing, Nell, and he said he doesn't believe God disapproves. He says God made him and loves him as he is and wants him to be happy," Sandy replied.

"I don't get it," Nell said, shaking her head.

"Sandy, why don't you and your husband come out to the lake house this weekend," offered Ben. "Bring your son and the other kids, too. It will help take your mind off everything to just have fun together for a couple of days."

"Things have changed, Ben. Having a weekend together as if nothing has happened only delays the inevitable. I'm beginning to wonder if anything about our relationship as a mother and son has been real. It's like there is this other person in his place I'm supposed to love—this person I don't even know. Yet, he is my son, and I do love him."

There was an awkward silence as each of Sandy's friends tried to think of something else to say. Sandy looked down and said sadly, "I just don't understand why God has let this happen."

"We'll be praying for you and your son," Haven offered.

The divisions between the different models of response aren't necessarily cut and dried; and because all the people there were Christians, each of their responses reflected at least some aspect of the spiritual response. However, it is still fairly easy to see that Scott and Robin were looking for a solution that involved changing Sandy's feelings (emotional response). Laurie tried to separate Sandy from the cause of the problem, by recommending she consider severing her relationship with her son for a while (surgical response). Kayla focused on managing the symptoms of Sandy's pain, by sharing the contact information for a medical provider who might prescribe something for anxiety or insomnia (chemical response).

Ethan focused on finding a solution that involved taking specific action to resolve the situation (behavioral response). Nell didn't really offer a solution, but commented in a way that revealed she was focusing on the religious aspects of the son's revelation (spiritual response). Samuel and Haven also addressed the problem by offering scriptural encouragement, prayer, and theological analysis (also spiritual response). Finally, Ben focused on improving happiness and harmony in the family, by suggesting Sandy do something that would make her happy and take her mind off the situation for a while (self-esteem response).

Haven later said she had noticed the signs of idolatry in Sandy's downcast face and anxious confusion; but she had not mentioned it, for fear of seeming condemning or uncaring. Unfortunately, none of Sandy's friends—as well intentioned as they were—provided any real help. Even if she were to implement their suggestions, God would not bless her efforts if they were an offering to the idol of her heart.

☙ ❧

The next morning, Sandy has coffee with her friend Iris, who helps her examine her heart for wrong worship (biblical model of response). As you read their conversation, notice how different Iris' responses are than the ones Sandy received the previous evening.

Note that, rather than try to ease Sandy's pain, help her feel better, tell her how to address the circumstances, or instruct her in behavioral change, Iris simply helps Sandy consider what desires she might be worshipping. This is important.

Later, Iris will help Sandy identify practical, godly ways to respond to her son; but she knows that until Sandy's heart is set more on God than on her own desires and fears, any practical advice she gives will be built on a shaky foundation. God alone is the ultimate source of the wisdom Sandy needs.

(Note that wherever there is scripture listed, Iris usually has Sandy read that scripture aloud and asks her what she thinks it means.)

"I can't find God's peace in this," Sandy began. "I'm so hurt and angry. I feel like my son has put me in the position of choosing between my love for him and my love for God."

"What do you mean?"

"If I reject this . . . development . . . I lose my son. It feels like a test, but I don't know who is testing me—my son or God. Maybe God is making me choose between Him or my son, the way He did with Abraham. All I know is that pretending something is okay, when I believe it dishonors God, feels like I'm denying the authority of God's Word. It's tearing me apart."

"What about the situation bothers you the most?" Iris asked gently.

"I want to be pleasing to God, and I know God commands us to love; but this isn't just a matter of saying, 'I love you.' It affects us in so many ways. How are we going to handle family gatherings? What if he asks us to come to his wedding? How will he respond if I don't go? How can I love him when the only love he will accept is one that embraces what I believe God says is sin? 'Woe to those who call sin, good,' the Bible says."

"Actually, it says, 'Woe to those who call evil, good' (Isaiah 5:20) and if you look at that verse in context, it is speaking of ignoring or denying the evil in our *own* heart and our own behavior. So, it is most important to consider your heart first, and whether you are worshipping God in this difficult situation . . . or something else."

"I *am* worshipping God."

"Yes and no. You *want* to worship God, but it sounds like your heart isn't experiencing His wisdom and comfort. It sounds like you're preoccupied with trying to figure out how to respond to your son. Your confusion, anxiety, and pain all point to something other than God as the focus of your worship, because God's peace is unconditional. It doesn't depend on circumstances. Maybe you're worshipping the desire that your son didn't have these attractions, that he had kept it secret or didn't live it out, that you had done something different in raising him, or that he hadn't put you in this difficult position. Any of those desires could be potential idols of your heart—things you feel must be in place in order for you to be at peace about the future."

"How about all of them . . . "

"It's important to know exactly what is being worshipped most, so you can accurately confess it. Would you like help figuring that out?"

"Sure."

"Okay, let's start with: What do you fear right now?"

"I fear having to pretend I'm okay with something I cannot bear. I fear the hypocrisy of 'being loving' when I feel only heartbreak and discomfort."

"I can understand that. How would you finish the following sentence? 'If only _________, then I could be okay.'"

"I would say, 'If only I could get my son to not go down this path,' but I know it's pointless. I can't control him, and he says this is just who he is. So, I guess I would say, 'If only I could figure out how to respond. If only I could get my son to understand how painful and difficult this is for me.'"

"So if you could help your son understand and knew you wouldn't lose him if you could be honest about your feelings, would you have some comfort?" Iris asked.

"Yes, but it feels like I've already lost him," Sandy said.

"How would you finish this sentence, 'After all I have done, you would think _______?'"

"I don't know."

"What would you guess?"

"That he would have turned out okay. We tried so hard. Where did we go wrong?"

"Sandy, do you see the possibility that your desire for things to be different might be an idol of your heart that you are worshipping and serving more than God?"

"No. It is because of my desire to please God that I am so upset."

"I understand, but your happiness should rest in the Lord, not in your son's attractions."

"So I'm supposed to just accept it and act like it's nothing?"

"You're still thinking about having to suffer the circumstances, not how you might honor God with every step you take in those circumstances. Spiritually speaking, idolatry is a matter of trying to be god of your own life. So, set your heart on God, first. He is faithful (1 Corinthians 1:9) and He will show you what to do. Trying to do the right thing from a wrong heart isn't God-honoring. Neither is waiting until you know what to do, before trusting God. You have to get your heart right and worship God *before* you have all the answers."

"But *how* do I get my heart right?"

"By asking God to remove whatever desire is holding your heart hostage. I know that sounds difficult, but it is important to understand that clinging to any desire is a form of idolatry—no matter how godly that desire might sound—and idolatry dishonors God. The Bible says even your prayers for your son won't be heard. 'Who may ascend the mountain of the LORD? Who may stand in His holy place? The one who has clean hands and a pure heart, who does not trust in an idol' (Psalm 24:3-4)."

"So, you're saying ask God to remove my desire for my son to be different, or for him to understand my feelings, or for me to be able to know how to love him without feeling like I'm demonstrating disregard for God's Word . . . where do I begin?"

"Whichever desire is the one that is most piercing and enslaving your heart right now is the one you should focus on. It sounds to me like the last one is causing the most heartache right now."

"But then what? I don't think I can ever accept what I believe dishonors God and is so unnatural," Sandy said, in obvious pain.

"Actually, it's 'natural' in mankind's sinful state to obey the inclinations and desires of the flesh. As believers, our bondage to sin is broken; but we are still flesh and bones (Galatians 5:17). Our hearts are still inclined to 'gratify the cravings of the flesh and follow its desires and thoughts' (Ephesians 2:1-5). That just happens to lead to different things for different people.

What is *unnatural* is obeying God's unique command to live according to His prescribed limits on our desires.[17] He alone gives us the ability to do so. By the power of the Holy Spirit, He gives us the desire to please Him more than we desire to please ourselves."

"That doesn't tell me what I'm supposed to do or how I'm supposed to interact with him and . . . his partner. It doesn't tell me how I'm supposed to demonstrate love, without setting aside my faith."

"You're trying to figure out by what rules you can control the future. Rest in the Lord and let Him guide you. 'Be anxious for nothing,' but in prayer and thanksgiving ask God to show you how to demonstrate a parent's love, without dishonoring God (Philippians 4:6). Thank Him for your son and the privilege of being his mother. Whatever you do, do it out of love for God, not to 'make your son feel loved' and not to 'be right' (1 Corinthians 16:14). Cling to Christ instead of your desires or fears, and He will give you peace and freedom from 'agitating passions or moral conflict' (James 3:18 AMP). Trust God and He will guide you in what to say and do."

Sandy confessed her desires as idolatrous and God's peace did come over her. No longer consumed with worries—about being consistent, making her son feel loved, speaking her mind, getting her son to change, wanting him to understand how hurt she was, or seeming godly—she was able to love her son without contradicting her desire to please God. Her efforts became fragrant offerings to the Lord, and God gave her the wisdom to navigate the difficult practical situations that arose along the way, in a manner that was pleasing to Him.

☙ ❧

Like Sandy, I also experienced a situation where it was difficult to know how to please God, and where my efforts to do so resulted in being rejected and condemned by nearly every member of my family. Each of them loved God, but none understood how I could put desiring to please Him above family unity or individual happiness. When I tried to explain, I was accused of being self-righteous and unchristlike.

Even in the midst of what would eventually become an eight-year struggle, I knew I was not entirely innocent. My "downcast face" and "tormenting spirit" told me I surely had idols hidden somewhere in my heart. It was easy to identify wanting to be loved and accepted by my family as one idol, but it would take several years to even *begin* seeing the others.

My first breakthrough came when I realized I was angry someone else's sin could disrupt my own spiritual peace. How brutally unfair it seemed that they were cheerfully going on with their lives, while I was being buffeted about in the wake of the destruction they left behind. The irony of worshipping an idol of "having spiritual peace" was not lost on me, given how much of my spiritual growth has come through spiritual struggle.

The second breakthrough came when the Holy Spirit showed me that my hurt at being called "unchristlike" by my family came from an idol of wanting to be considered a woman after God's heart. That was pride, nothing else, and seeing it was like looking at the back of my gown to find it torn and covered in filth.

I repented of those things and gained a measure of peace, but I could tell it was not truly God's peace. As the holidays approached, I grew increasingly anxious about upcoming family events—as terrified I might displease God by worshipping the desire for reconciliation or acceptance, as by failing to adequately *seek* that reconciliation.

Crying out to God, I felt His assurance that He knew how much I wanted to please Him and would protect me from any situation where I would not know how to do so. Such a thing had never occurred to me before. Yet, over the next eighteen months, every time I felt anxious about an event, it was changed in some way so I no longer had cause for concern.

Then, one day, that assurance was replaced by God's quiet reminder that I need not be anxious at all, for He would guide me in what to say or do, exactly when I needed to know (Matthew 10:19). My fears were gone, new opportunities to interact with my family arose, and the first gentle signs of healing began to take place.

Just a few weeks later, however, everything was thrown into turmoil again by a family lawsuit I could not in good conscience support. I had agreed to be the only witness for the opposing side, knowing full well the price I would pay; but remaining silent was not an option. To do so would have been to participate in injustice for the self-serving goal of keeping my family's love. The precept of being willing to lose mother, father, sister, and brother to become a follower Christ (Luke 12:46) soon became very real and personal.

I was blocked from social media, disinvited to every family event or celebration, and written off as dead by much of my family. I was willing to ask forgiveness, if I could figure out what to ask forgiveness for. It was impossible for me to deny that, given the choice between pleasing God or pleasing family, I would choose what I felt was most pleasing to God—even if it meant losing my family's affection. To my family, however, the two were nearly synonymous. Families stuck together. Period.

Trying to explain the reason for my position (behavioral response) only made things worse. So, I consoled myself emotionally (emotional response), withdrew from my family (surgical response), and invested time in people who made me feel accepted and loved (self-esteem response). Daily, I prayed (spiritual response) for God to "create in me a clean heart and renew in me a right spirit" (biblical response, Psalm 51:10). Daily, He helped me love and forgive. Yet, I could still feel sin "crouching at the door, desiring to have me" (Genesis 4:7) with temptations to self-pity and bitterness.

Over the next eight months I continually weighed all these things in my heart. Then one evening, I felt the Holy Spirit chastise me for leaning so much on my own understanding (Proverbs 3:5-6). I was trying to figure everything out, so I could go to God at my best. He wanted me to come to Him at my worst—failing in self-sufficiency, confused by idolatry, saddened by rejection, and desperately aware of my need for His wisdom, love, and mercy.

> *Come to me, all who labor and are heavy laden, and I will give you rest (Matthew 11:28).*

The Holy Spirit then showed me that my spiritual journey was not the gentle, upward-winding road I had imagined it to be, marked by occasional potholes of difficulty to overcome. Rather, it was a series of stepping-stones, with those difficulties the very means by which God was doing His work in me. I had been looking on them with resentment, when I should have been looking on them with the curiosity of an interested student facing a difficult and challenging class.

> *Do not regard lightly the discipline of the Lord, nor be weary when reproved by him. For the Lord disciplines the one he loves (Hebrews 12:5-6a).*

So, I relinquished the idolatrous longing for resolution and embraced the opportunity to practice patience in suffering. I relinquished the idolatrous desire for acceptance and embraced the challenge of seeking to please God without giving way to sin. I relinquished the idolatrous need to "be right" and embraced the idea that God was surely working in the rest of my family as much as He was working in me. I stopped striving and started learning to wait "in the limbo" of trusting the Lord.

Months later, as I was sharing with my small group at church all that had taken place, tears unexpectedly came to my eyes. Suddenly, I could see how double-minded I had been in proclaiming a desire to be reconciled with my family, while doubting it was possible . . . or even desirable. Repenting in my heart, I was immediately filled with such wholehearted love for two of the estranged family members that all my previous efforts to willfully love them seemed determined and shallow.

Those two relationships were miraculously restored three days later, through circumstances none of us could have planned or imagined. I was delighted, but confused. Why had God given me such deep love for only two and not the other three? Why were just those reconciled and not the others? Was I waiting on Him or was He waiting on me?

Several more months passed. Then one afternoon, at the end of a day-long counseling lecture, I invited my students to spend the last few minutes of class, role-playing counseling situations. Pairing up with one of the newest students, I offered myself as the "counselee," and my family situation as the topic. Neither of us expected much to come from the short exercise.

"Um," she said hesitantly in her role-play as counselor, "how would you describe the perfect family?"

I felt like I had been hit with a spiritual 2 x 4. It was such an obvious and important question, yet I had never even thought to ask it of myself. A hundred possible answers flew through my mind in seconds, and I could only stammer I would have to give it some thought. I encouraged her to ask another.

"Okay . . . hmm, is there anything you regret?"

Another spiritual 2 x 4 crashed into my conscience. *Of course* there were things I regretted. The fact that they were not sinful, in themselves, didn't matter. I could see how they still darkened my conscience. When I repented, the full force of God's peace rushed in.

The verse about Christ being present when two or more are gathered in His name (Matthew 18:20) came alive for me that day, in a new way. The Holy Spirit had accomplished more in my heart through someone who, by her own admission, "had no idea what she was doing," than I had accomplished in more than *eight years of self-counseling.* Training and experience are not enough. We really need each other, for it is Christ among us who changes lives.

A few months later—again through unexpected circumstances—the three remaining relationships were also miraculously restored. Due to distance and time, we may never be as close as I would like; but I have God's peace. The former anger and heartache are gone (Psalm 103:12); and though I still grieve sin and the destruction it causes, that godly grief is now well-balanced with godly love.

ᴄᴧ ᴥ ᴄᴧ ᴥ

Chapter 9- Homework

1. List the seven models of response for dealing with unhappiness and try to think of a situation from your life for which each one would be appropriate.

2. Which model of response do you tend to gravitate toward, when faced with a problem, or when helping someone else?

3. Based on your responses and the way you think about problems, which worldview do you think you hold?

4. Have you found yourself hoping that by emptying your heart of idols, you could be more righteous? What temptations or dangers are inherent in that thought?

5. Think of a situation that happened this week (perhaps something less painful than the one you chose for this study) and describe what it might look like to respond to that situation from each of the seven models of response.

Chapter 9 - Prayer

Lord God,

Almighty God, whose name is the Lord of hosts, great in counsel and mighty in deed, You made the heavens and the earth by Your great power and by Your outstretched arm. You made and fashioned me. Help me to embrace your love. Teach me what it means to fear You for my own good, that I might not turn away from You. Give me understanding that I will delight in obeying Your commandments, for You are righteous. Comfort me with Your steadfast love and fill my heart with Your praise (from Jeremiah 32:17, 39 and Psalm 119:73-80). In Jesus' name, amen.

Journal

In this study, you are learning to apply the biblical model of response to all situations. Explain how each of the models of response might apply to the issue you have chosen to explore for this study. Which ones have you already tried? Which ones have you applied incorrectly and which ones correctly? Do you think the biblical response *could* be accurately applied to your situation? Why or why not? Do you have a sense of trying to control? Have you slipped into misapplying the biblical response?

10. Listening Questions

The Bible says, "To give an answer before listening is foolish" (Proverbs 18:13); and one of the best ways to listen well is by asking good questions. The Listening Questions below are ones I use when helping others and also what I ask of myself when I'm examining my own heart.

There's nothing deeply theological about these particular questions; they're just helpful for listening to the heart's emotional and spiritual motivations, the way a stethoscope is useful for listening to a heart's physical sounds. Their purpose isn't to gather facts, but to provide opportunities for the heart to speak so that the signs or symptoms of idolatry, if any, might be revealed.

Resist the temptation to presume you already know the answers and ask each question with genuine curiosity—as if you knew nothing about human emotions or motivations. Make it your goal to really listen and hear, rather than figure out and fix. The Holy Spirit will begin to reveal things as clearly as if He were counseling that person with you if you leave room for Him to do so. Don't ignore tears. When they come unexpectedly, it often means God has softened the person's heart and preparing them for wonderful repentance.

Listening Questions

A. "What about (the situation) specifically bothers you most (makes you unhappy, afraid, angry, etc.)?"

Rushing to express sympathy for a painful situation may seem kind, but as soon as you say, "I'm so sorry," you have effectively ended the conversation. What else is there to say? On the other hand, asking to know *why* a situation hurts is an expression of a willingness to listen further.

Variations of this question might include: "Why does that upset you, specifically?" or "That would make me sad, too, but perhaps for different reasons—what specifically about it saddens you?" It might seem hurtful or even silly to ask someone those questions; but in the right tone of voice, it is a thoughtful invitation to share desires or concerns they might not otherwise feel comfortable sharing.

Say, for example, a counselee's spouse has committed adultery. What bothers her most might be the betrayal and lies, the disruption to the children's lives, or the fear of never being loved again. She might even say it is the financial concerns. *You* might think it's because she's afraid of being alone, or because she doesn't want to dishonor God. You have to ask.

Of course, the practical matters of adultery are important and deserving of biblical advice, but an exploration of the heart should always come first. As long as there is idolatry—which there always is whenever God's peace is lacking—it will be impossible to implement even the best practical advice with the wisdom and peace of God. At best, whatever is tried will have no impact. At worst, it will magnify the problem and add to it.

B. "If that were to true . . . what about it would bother you the most?"

When someone says, "I'm so worried that____________," or "I'm so afraid that ____________," our initial tendency is to either minimize those fears in an effort to make the person feel better or put on our detective hats and try to determine whether those fears or suspicions are justified. Both distract from the more important issue of looking for the underlying idol of the heart—the deep desire, which that fear threatens most.

One way to do this is to have the frightened or worried person presume that what they fear *has* come true, or is already true, and then ask what about being in that circumstance or situation upsets them most. Don't presume you already know. Even if you are right, you might be surprised by the specifics.

You could ask, *"Based on what you've told me, it sounds possible that (what is suspected) may be true . . . If it were, what about that would bother you most?"* Other versions might be: *"If_____ were to happen, what about it would bother you?"* or, *"Suppose _____ were already true, what about that would bother you most?"* The response is usually a sigh of relief at being allowed to fully explore those fears, rather than having to justify having them.

C. "What would you guess?"

When a person can't think of an answer to a particular question, you can ask them to guess what their answer might be. It's amazing how much is revealed by that simple invitation.

You can even invite *yourself* to "guess" about your own feelings, when asking yourself these questions.

It may sound odd, but the invitation to guess is good for general conversation, too. When my husband seems lost in thought and I ask, "What are you thinking about?" he almost always answers, "Nothing." If I then say, "If you were to guess, what would it be?" he usually has much to say.

D. "Can you give me an example?" "What do you mean?"

When a person says something general like, "My husband doesn't communicate," "My child is so disrespectful," or, "My wife is always depressed," ask for an example. If they use a broad term like "always," "never," "too much," or "not enough," ask what they mean. Generalities are summaries that rely on presumption for their effect, deflecting attention away from the areas of the heart where the idols are found.

For example, a woman who says "My husband drinks too much," might be displeased with his behavior when he drinks, irrespective of the quantity he drinks; or she might be upset because he drinks at all—or drinks more than a certain amount she feels is acceptable—irrespective of his behavior. It is important to know her underlying motivation, because a woman whose happiness depends on her husband not drinking has a completely different idol than one whose happiness depends on her husband behaving well, when he drinks.

Your effort to understand which one she is worshipping, is not so you can help her change her husband, but so you can help her take that idolatrous desire to God and ask Him to remove it. *Then*, you can then help her with practical, biblical advice for addressing the situation with her husband, should she still feel the need to do so.

E. "Can we role-play a typical scenario that upsets you?"

I frequently offer to role-play a specific, typical interaction or scenario someone has described, with myself taking one side and them taking the other. If possible, we stand and actually walk it out; but seated works just as well. It doesn't matter whether I play the hurting person or the opposing person.

Whenever there is a problem between two people, it's almost certain *both* are in idolatry and seeking to please themselves. Given a few details, it's not at all difficult to imagine what that would look like. The surprising accuracy of these impromptu and unscripted role-plays helps a person realize their situation is not as unique as they imagined it to be, and that there is more going on spiritually than meets the eye.

F. "You mentioned that . . ."

Random comments that appear to have little to do with the narrative could be "escaped" heart-expressions of idols hidden behind that narrative. This tends to happen most often, when a great deal of self-analysis or professional counseling has already taken place, such that the problem or issue is neatly packaged and thoroughly analyzed.

For example, a young woman named Tabitha offered to volunteer to participate in a demonstration of the Listening Questions. In particular, she wanted to explore her heart regarding "demonic-like dreams" she had been having about harm coming to her young children.

Several different desires and fears were shared, but none that seemed to be dominating her heart. Even the concern something might happen to her children was quite easily given to God. There was simply no sign of idolatry, and none of the Listening Questions revealed any. It felt like we were going in circles—discussing the same thoughts and feelings again and again in a very honest, but almost superficial way.

Tabitha had made several, seemingly unrelated, comments about being certain God was going to give her a speaking ministry and feeling unworthy of the calling. She was adamantly determined, she said, not to pursue such a ministry for herself—it would have to come from other people inviting her. Not coincidentally, she had become very close to three women who had lost children in tragic accidents—each of whom was frequently asked to speak and share their testimony about experiencing God's comfort and peace in tragedy.

Although she never specifically stated it, it soon became clear that Tabitha's conviction God's plan for her to have a speaking ministry included the possibility of suffering some tragic event in her children's lives, just as it had for her friends. She even said she wasn't sure if she should pray God's protection over her children or surrender herself to "His will." When I pointed out the possible connection, Tabitha saw it immediately. The demonic-like dreams stopped that night.

The next week, I suggested to Tabitha that the real problem might be that desiring to be a women's ministry speaker could have become an idol in her heart. She admitted listening "obsessively" to famous women's ministry leaders and trying to emulate them. She also said she frequently hinted to people in authority that, although she felt unworthy, she would speak if asked to do so. Both seemed like efforts to Control for Success, but she was afraid that confessing her desire as an idol might keep it from ever coming about.

Tabitha has a wonderful testimony of how God healed her from a very painful childhood and I could easily see her impacting the lives of many women as an inspiring and engaging ministry speaker. If she is indeed worshipping that desire, however, she will never fully experience the things God may have in store for her in that area.

G. "What do you think it might mean if ____________ were true? "

This question is similar to the one asking what would bother a person most if something were true, but this one asks what that person thinks it would *mean* if what they feared was true. This is almost always followed by asking whether or not they believe that conclusion is true.

H. "Do you believe that (conclusion) is true?"

Unlike all the other questions, this one has a "yes" or "no" answer. It is helpful for clearing away false beliefs that give rise to idolatrous fears, and refocus a person on what is really true. The response is often, *"No, I know it's not true; it's just that ______."* Then, you can inquire about that newly expressed fear or desire and see where it leads. If the response is, *"Yes, I do believe it is true,"* ask what about it being true bothers them the most. This is just one of many excellent places to offer scripture related to their particular fear.

I. "What about that made you feel teary, just now?"

Tears are almost always a cause for rejoicing, for they often mean God is standing at the door of the temple of a person's heart where their idol is hidden, and the possibility of repentance is near. It is terrifying to feel God's presence in an area that has been guarded and protected for so long and so carefully—and know God requires that cherished desire be relinquished and no longer worshipped. Rather than pretend to not notice the tears or rush to soothe them, ask, "What made you feel teary just now?"

If they're not willing to let God in, they will shut the door of their heart, and the tears will go away as quickly as they came. If they are willing, however, He will come in and time will seem to stand still in the presence of His holiness. The idols will crumble and evaporate, and that person's entire countenance will change. It is an incredible thing to witness.

Recognizing an idol intellectually might lead to verbal repentance, but not to that kind of life transformation. When God is involved, there is a visible and unmistakable element of awe, surprise, and deep humility.

J. "Is there anything you regret about your part in the situation?"

This can be powerful in helping someone step away from the trap of religious justification or intellectual analysis, and get to the underlying heart issues.

K. "Is there anything else?"

You can ask this question at any time—and *should* ask it if there's been no indication God is moving in the conversation.

It not only opens the door to unexpected areas you might have neglected by assumption; it also provides an opportunity for the hurting person to share things they thought were too insignificant or even embarrassing to mention, but are actually quite important. "Is there anything else separating you from the peace of God?" is another way to ask this.

L. "Do you have any regrets about the situation?"

I did not initially have this question on my list, but it was so powerful in the mock counseling session discussed at the end of Chapter 9 that I include it now in much of my own counseling.

ଓ ଃ

The following conversation demonstrates how a caring friend, who has no familiarity with the concept of idolatry, might respond to someone sharing a difficult situation regarding her marriage. See if you can identify the symptoms of idolatry in Pat's words, and the models of response Liz offers:

"I think I'm going to file for divorce," Pat said.

"Wow, Pat, what happened?" Liz asked.

"I'm just tired of trying so hard to make things work. My husband watches violent television in front of the kids, spends his evenings and weekends playing video games or on the Internet, and yells at the kids and me all the time. He never works on the house and it's falling down around us. When he gets mad, he disappears to his hunting cabin and gets drunk. Sometimes he stays there for a couple of days without even letting us know." Pat continued describing other difficulties she has had with her husband. Then she said, "I've tried everything, but nothing is changing and I'm fed up. I can't believe God wants me to suffer like this.

"That's a lot! I had no idea things were so bad. Have you tried ________? Maybe if you_______." Liz offered several suggestions for things Pat could do or say.

"I've tried all that. You wouldn't believe the sacrifices I've made."

"Are you sure there's nothing else you could do? Have you prayed about it?"

"I've prayed and prayed, but nothing has changed. Either God doesn't hear or He doesn't care about me. I've stuck it out for the children for ten years, but they're grown now. Even being alone the rest of my life would be better than this."

"So, what are you going to do?

"I have an appointment with my attorney this Friday. I'm going to find out what my options are, but I imagine I'll go ahead with divorce."

"Does your husband know?"

"No, but I'm going to tell him tonight."

"I wish you didn't have to do this. Isn't there is a chance you two could work it out? Have you seen a counselor?"

"I have, but he refused to go."

"Do you still love your husband?" Liz asked.

"Right now? No. Maybe I never did. I think I just felt pressured to get married."

"Oh Pat, I'm so sorry. I'll be praying for you."

Liz's response is typical of most Christian friends. To her credit, she doesn't sin by gossiping about Pat's husband, but she really has no idea what to say to help Pat. She believes God's Word to be true. She just isn't sure how to apply that truth to helping others.

When you consider their dialogue from a worship perspective, it's easy to see Pat is looking at her situation from a self-protective position above the one-way mirror of the Idols Chart. She is only able to see three things: her pain, what her husband is doing to contribute to that pain, and how hard she has struggled in trying to respond.

The symptoms of a tormenting spirit and downcast face are evident, as is the fact that her heart has become hardened as self-protection against further pain. Believing a happy marriage is impossible even with God, Pat has decided it would be less painful to destroy any hope of having a happy marriage with her husband, than continue in the unfulfilled longing for it.

> *Hope deferred makes the heart sick, but a longing fulfilled is a tree of life (Proverbs 13:12).*

It's not that Pat can't bear another moment with her husband. She just can't bear another moment of the heartache of not being able to get him to change. That may seem like an insignificant difference, but it's not. Change is what she wants, and if her husband were to change even a little in the ways she desired—before she commits to divorce—she would probably prefer to continue in the marriage. The change wouldn't have to be complete. It would just have to be enough to give her hope.

What Pat doesn't realize is that she is worshipping the desire for her husband to change, and that idol has separated her from God's blessings in her marriage. Even if God *did* change her husband, she wouldn't enjoy those blessings. On the other hand, if she truly relinquishes her trust in what she wants and puts her trust in God, He will move in their marriage in a way that deeply blesses her. That may not make sense or even seem possible, but it is spiritual truth.

> *Seek first the kingdom of God and His righteousness, and all these things will be added to you (Matthew 6:33).*

☙ ❧

The next day Pat has lunch with Jan, who has been studying idols of the heart and applying the concepts to her own life. Notice that Jan doesn't get distracted by the details of the husband's sin or frightened by the prospect of divorce. She might later give Pat some practical, biblical tools for interacting with her husband, but first she just listens. Then, she helps Pat examine her heart through a biblical lens of worship.

(Of necessity, the conversation has been condensed. It would normally take place over an hour or two):

"I think I'm going to file for divorce," Pat said.

"Wow, Pat, what happened?" Jan asked.

"I'm just tired of trying so hard to make things work. My husband watches violent television in front of the kids, spends all his time at home playing video games or on the Internet, and yells at kids and me all the time. He never works on the house and it's falling down around us. When he gets mad, he disappears to his hunting cabin and gets drunk.

Sometimes he stays there for a couple of days without even letting us know." Pat continued describing other difficulties she has had with her husband. Then she said, "I've tried everything, but nothing is changing and I'm fed up. I can't believe God wants me to suffer like this."

"That's a lot! I had no idea things were so bad. May I ask which of those things bothers you the most?"

"Everything."

"If you had to choose, what would you guess?"

"I'd say all the yelling and getting drunk and disappearing when he's mad. It's unbearable."

"Can you give me an example?"

"Yesterday, all I did was ask when he was going to fix the fence. He cursed at me in front of the kids, grabbed a case of beer, and left."

"That would upset me, too, but maybe for different reasons. What about it bothered *you* the most?"

"That he makes it impossible to discuss anything. I know no one is perfect, but at least for the sake of the children, he could try."

"Try what, exactly?" Jan asked with curiosity.

"To do better," Pat explained. "If he would just talk to me and listen. It would at least show he cared. That's all I've ever asked.

"Okay, bear with me: what bothers you the most about him not seeming to care?"

"That he *should* care!" Pat said, with frustration. "We don't spend any time together. We don't communicate, and even when I try, he just tunes me out and leaves."

"What are you afraid it might mean when he does that?"

"That he doesn't love me," Pat replied.

"Do you believe that is true?"

"No. But I don't *feel* loved."

"What would you like to see happen?" Jan asked. "For example, how would you fill in this sentence: *'If only ________, then I'd be happy'?"*

"I know it sounds terrible, but I almost wish he would have an affair, so I could divorce him without feeling guilty."

"The Bible doesn't say adultery is grounds for divorce."

"My sister says it does."

"It says that a person who divorces for any reason other than adultery and remarries is an adulterer (Matthew 19:9), that a man who divorces his wife makes her an adulteress, unless she already is one; and that a man who marries a divorced woman is an adulterer (Matthew 5:32)."

"So, are you saying that even if he had an affair, I couldn't leave him?"

"What I'm saying is that looking for exemptions to a law is just a reverse form of legalism. You'll either judge yourself righteous for staying *despite* his sin, or judge yourself justified in leaving *because* of it. Either way, you will have taken God's place as Judge."

"So, it *is* okay for me to divorce him?"

"Getting a divorce won't send you to hell any more than not getting one will make you righteous; but it *will* cause you to miss out on experiencing God working in your marriage—and I would hate for you to miss that."

"It's hopeless. I've already tried."

"Perhaps that's because your motivation has been wrong. God doesn't bless efforts that are really just an offering or sacrifice to get what you desire. You said yourself it feels like God isn't hearing your prayers."

Pat sighed. "I just don't know what to do any more."

"Let me ask again, then, what would you put in the statement: 'If only ______, then I'd be happy'?"

"I suppose if he quit watching violent TV shows when the kids were home, quit playing video games or being on the Internet, quit yelling, and got the house fixed up."

"Okay, let's test that. If he did all those things, but he still didn't talk to you, listen, or seem to care about you and the marriage—would you be happy?"

"I guess so. Sure. Maybe." She shrugged and then changed her mind. "No," she said, shaking her head sadly.

"Okay, so what if he didn't change at all in those areas; but he started caring, took time to listen and talk, and let you know he loves you . . . how about then?"

"I'd still want him to change, but I could deal with all the other things if I knew he loved me and cared about our marriage."

"A minute ago you said you wanted to divorce him and didn't love him. You even hoped he would have an affair, so you could. Why does the idea of him not loving you bother you now?"

"I want to love him, and I want him to love me. I just can't bear being in a marriage without love."

"And if you can't have that, you are willing to divorce?"

"That's right."

"It sounds like your real desire is for a loving marriage, not divorce."

"Well, yes, but I don't think it's going to happen."

"Only God knows, but it's important to identify your real desire. If it's for a loving marriage, then your real hope is for God to restore your marriage."

"So, I *shouldn't* file?" Pat asked.

"Staying in your marriage with a bitter and self-pitying heart is no more godly than leaving it. The 'outside of the cup' might look clean, but the inside would still be filthy. Jesus says clean the inside first, and then the outside will also be clean." [18]

"How do I do that?"

"May I show you something?" Jan asked.

"Sure," Pat replied.

Jan drew a simple Idols Chart, shared James 1:15, and gave Pat some examples of common idols. Then she helped her consider possible idolatry in her own situation.

"Wanting your husband to change the things he does could be an idol of your heart. But you said even if those things did change, you would still be unhappy if you didn't feel loved by him. That's why I said it sounds like your main desire is for your husband to be more loving," Jan said.

"Is that wrong?" Pat asked.

"Only in that you have made your happiness dependent on it coming about," Jan replied. "Your happiness should depend on God, and your trust for the future should rest in your confidence of God's authority and sovereignty, not in your husband changing. God surely desires for your husband to love you; but when you began worshipping that desire, you made it an idol and separated yourself from God's power, peace, and blessing. Maybe your prayers for your husband aren't being answered because they are really just prayers for God to worship your idol with you."

"Do you think God is punishing me?"

"What do you mean?"

"Because we had sex before we got married, and I married an unbeliever. Maybe God *wants* me to get divorced, so I won't be 'unequally yoked' anymore."

"If you weren't married, we could talk about God's desires for you as a single woman, or His will for you in choosing a husband. There are consequences to not trusting God, just as there are blessings to trusting Him. But you can't correct a previous lack of trust by mistrusting Him again. You can best honor God now, by pleasing Him in the situation as it is, not by trying to undo it. If you believe 'God works in *all* things for the good of those who love Him and are called according to His purpose' (Romans 8:28), you can start by trusting God now."

"What do you mean?"

"You trusted your own desires more than God's Word in the past. It didn't work out very well. Do you still trust your own desires more, or do you want to trust God?"

"I just want to be happy. But I do trust God. I wouldn't have survived in my marriage this long if I didn't."

"But you have also been trusting the idea of being happy and made your happiness dependent on getting your husband to change. You've been worshipping happiness."

"So, God *is* punishing me."

"Try to think of God withholding His blessing as 'discipline,' rather than punishment. If He blessed your idolatry, you would just worship idols more—and the end of idolatry is death. He wants you to stop, recognize the sin that's there, and return to Him."

"But God commands my husband to love me and sacrifice himself for me, 'as Christ did for the church.'"

"That's true, but God's commands for you are not dependent on whether your husband obeys God's commands for him."

"Well, what he is doing affects me."

"There is nothing your husband is doing that can separate you from God's blessings. Only the sin in your own heart can do that. May I show you what I mean?"

"Okay."

Jan pointed to the Idols Chart. "Let's put the desire for your husband to love you at the bottom of this chart, on the left. What emotions or behavior, what 'fruit,' is coming out of that desire?"

Suddenly sad, Pat said, "I guess the things I've been doing. Complaining, criticizing, manipulating, controlling, being bossy, envying other women's husbands, self-righteousness."

"And what has been the result of that? Has your husband become more godly or caring? Have you become happier? Are you at peace?"

"I see your point. But I was trying to do the right thing."

"If your motivation for trying to please God is to get something you have already decided you must have, it is self-serving, not God-serving."

"All my effort was just a sacrifice to an idol—is that right?"

"Yes, and the only appropriate sacrifice since Christ died for us, is a 'sacrifice of praise' (Hebrews 13:15)—with a humble, contrite and broken heart (Psalm 51:17)."

"My heart is definitely broken."

"Yes, but your heart is broken because of your husband's sin. God is looking for a heart contrite and broken because of its *own* sin," Janet replied, gently.

"So, I'm not supposed to care what my husband does?"

"If the desire you relinquish as an idol is part of God's plan for you, He will purify it and give it back to you in some form. You can still care about your husband growing in godliness and pray for him, you just can't worship that hope."

"I'm scared. I feel like if I stop wanting my husband to change, God won't change him."

Jan smiled. "So you're saying your husband is more powerful than God? You don't need to be afraid. God's will is always good and perfect and pleasing. He always blesses those whose hearts are set on Him." Noticing tears forming in Pat's eyes, she asked, "What is making you feel teary just now?

"I don't know."

"Can you guess?"

"I feel like it's all my fault.

"Pat, your husband is responsible for his sin and you are responsible for yours. Your marriage is just the stage on which God is revealing Himself to you and working in your faith. Take your mind off the past and focus on pleasing God today. He is able to turn things around in an instant, and use each of your past sins for His glory."

"What do I need to do?"

"Ask God to remove the idol of having your husband's love. Then pray for your husband, and delight in seeking to please God more than you delight in anything else. Relinquish all bitterness and self-pity, and ask God to fill your heart with love for your husband. He will."

Pat prayed, "Lord, I confess I have made an idol out of having my husband's love for me and ask You to remove that idol from my heart. Today I put my trust in You. Give me a heart that is pure and delights in pleasing You. Fill me with love for my husband and show me how I can serve You in my marriage. Restore our marriage, that it will be a testimony of praise to You. Amen."

Afterward, Pat told Jan she felt like a huge burden had been lifted from her heart and replaced with incredible peace. Her love for her husband began to grow, as did his love for her. Later that year, she marveled at how happy their marriage had become. She couldn't say for sure whether she or her husband had changed more, but things between them were definitely different. She would say they were "better," but that seemed too clinical. "Deeper and richer" was a more accurate description.

> *Commit your way to the Lord; trust in Him, and He will act (Psalm 37:5).*

Jan met with Pat several more times to share practical, biblical wisdom for how to honor God in her marriage.[19] It is sometimes helpful to give practical advice first, if a person needs an opportunity to experience God's faithfulness before addressing their heart. However, the heart should always be explored at some point—as well as the Gospel. Otherwise, it's a bit like giving someone a recipe for baking cookies, before helping them check to see if their oven is properly working.

10. Listening Questions

ᴄᴃ ᴆᴐ

You don't have to know all the right things to say or ask, before you can help someone else biblically. Neither do you have to have a degree in counseling or be an expert. Biblical counseling is discipleship and evangelism. Keep your heart on God rather than the circumstances, share the Gospel, ask questions, listen carefully, and frame your responses in terms of heart worship. God will do the rest.

Natalie and Elaine had met as roommates at a conference on idols of the heart, the year after Natalie's twin brother committed suicide. When Natalie learned Elaine had also lost a sibling to suicide, she was thankful to have found someone who could understand the pain of her loss.

"Do you think I have made my brother my idol?" Natalie asked during a walk between sessions on the second day of the conference. "Every time I think of him, I still cry."

"I don't know, Elaine said. "I've wondered myself if I have an idol about my sister."

"My grief is almost greater than I can bear," Natalie confessed. "I'm angry with my brother and angry with God. I don't understand why He let this happen, and I don't know what to do. Why am I even here at this conference? I don't know what I believe anymore. If God is a loving God, why did He let my brother kill himself?"

In the past, Elaine might have said, "I'm so sorry. I felt the same way when my sister died. I'll be praying for you." Instead she offered to ask Natalie some of the Idols Test and Listening Questions.

"Sure," Natalie answered.

"Umm . . . okay," Elaine began, trying to remember what they had learned to ask. "What would you say you needed in order to be happy?"

"For my brother to still be alive," Natalie answered.

"This feels awkward to ask," Elaine said, "but 'what grieves you the most about his dying?'"

"Everything. I don't know where to begin."

"What would you guess?"

"I guess the way he died. It still would have been awful if he had died in an accident, but suicide? How could I have missed the signs? We were so close and we told each other everything. Sure, we argued a lot, but never hatefully. We could discuss anything and still love each other. I miss him so much."

They walked a while in silence. "What is most difficult about him being gone?" Elaine asked with compassion.

Natalie thought a moment before answering. "Knowing I'll never have that kind of friendship again with anyone else. People who aren't twins don't understand the bond. I can't explain it." she wiped her eyes.

"I know what you mean," Elaine said. "It makes me so sad when I think about the bond my sister and I had, too." Stopping, she turned and asked, "But what made you feel teary just now, about not having that any longer with your brother?"

"Because what we had is gone now, and I can't bear it," Natalie said, as she started to cry.

Elaine put a hand on Natalie's shoulder to comfort her. Natalie took a deep breath and they began to walk again. "I feel strange asking this, but what about having had that kind of relationship for a while, not having it anymore, and possibly never having it again, is making you feel most sad?"

"I don't know," Natalie replied.

"If you were to guess . . .?"

"Maybe that I didn't really appreciate him enough when he was alive. Maybe because I didn't see how much he was hurting. I am so confused. Why didn't he tell me? I knew he was feeling down, but that wasn't unusual. Why didn't he let me know he was thinking of killing himself?"

"What are you afraid his not telling you might mean?"

Natalie thought for a minute, then answered, "Maybe it means he felt like he couldn't talk to me. I loved him, but sometimes I got tired of how argumentative he could be . . . and he was so stubborn. The morning he died, I had stopped by to bring him something and we ended up in an argument. I don't even remember what I said when I left—just that I had to get to work and didn't have time for arguing. He called later, but I was in a meeting and didn't answer. Then he texted me, telling me he was sorry for making me angry and how bad he felt about that . . . but he always does that. I didn't think it meant he was going to kill himself."

"Is there anything else?"

"I can't stop wondering what would have happened if I had just answered the phone. I could have stepped away from my meeting. I could have at least replied to his text and told him I forgave him. Elaine, I don't know if I can ever forgive myself for not being there for him when he needed me."

"I'm not minimizing your pain in any way, but I know it is possible to grieve the death of someone we love without being paralyzed by guilt."

"But it's my fault. I shouldn't have gotten so angry or ignored him. If I had returned his call or gone back to see him, he would probably be alive now. It was so stupid and self-centered of me!"

They turned and started walking back toward the church for the afternoon session. Elaine thought for a moment, then asked, "Suppose you had answered your phone. What then?"

"I'd probably be irritated at him for calling me at work. He was always doing that, and my boss had already given me a warning. You can't imagine how hard it was to have to choose between my brother and my job all the time. I knew he was going to call—he always does after we fight—and I guess I was mad at him. I remember thinking how selfish he was for not respecting my need to work. Now I realize *I'm* the selfish one. Who cares about a job? At least he would still be alive."

"Even if you had left work and gone to talk to him, you would have had to go back at some point."

"I know, but it might have made a difference."

"Would you be grieving any differently about his death if you *had* talked to him and he seemed okay after a while, but killed himself anyway, after you left?"

"I'd still feel horrible."

"Suppose you were in a place where you couldn't have answered your phone, like on a flight."

"I'd feel bad for not having been available, but not as guilty as I do now for not answering."

"So, maybe your feelings of guilt are less for not answering, than for your *reasons* for not answering."

"That's probably true. It was selfish and self-centered of me to ignore his calls and texts. He was my brother."

"So do you remember that Idols Chart we learned about? Could wishing you had not been selfish, angry, or self-centered that day be an idol of your heart right now?"

"Maybe. But how am I supposed to stop feeling guilty for not being there for him? It would feel like I didn't care that he killed himself."

"Would that be true? Would you really not care?"

"No. I would still care."

"Could reminding yourself how selfish you think you were, be an effort to try to keep you from being selfish in the future?" Elaine offered.

"So you agree I was selfish and self-centered?"

"I'm not saying that. It's just what you've said, and what's going on in *your* heart is the important thing, right?"

"I guess I'm afraid if I stop feeling guilty, I might be selfish and cause some other horrible thing to happen."

"So, you're trying to control your sin by will power," Elaine smiled, adding teasingly, "*that* always works."

"Right," Natalie agreed, smiling and nodding. "I think that *is* what I'm trying to do."

"If your guilt really is a self-inflicted punishment or sacrifice for being selfish—as you see it—then maybe your vow to never be selfish again is like an offering."

"Oh my gosh, yes!" Natalie said, as she stopped and turned to look at Elaine in surprise.

"In a way, it sounds like you're trying to pay a penalty for wrongdoing, attaching guilt to yourself as a penalty," Elaine said softly, "or a sort of penance."

"You might be right," Natalie replied.

"You know Jesus already paid the price for our sin. Why don't you try asking God if the desire to 'have behaved differently' that day has become an idol—sort of your heart's effort to control. Then ask Him to remove that desire from your heart,"

"I'm sort of uncomfortable with that. It feels wrong to *not* feel guilty. Like I don't care."

"But if that guilt has become a form of worship, it is separating you from God's comfort."

"I will still be sad and miss my brother."

"Even Jesus grieved (John 11:35, Luke 19:41). But with your heart free of idolatry, I am sure the Holy Spirit will guide you in how to grieve the loss of your brother in a way that honors his life *and* glorifies God. He knows your grief[20] and will give you comfort."

"I believe that," Natalie said.

"And the comfort He gives you will enable you to comfort others" (2 Corinthians 1:3-5).

Natalie smiled at that thought. They stopped walking and stood together as Natalie prayed. Hugging Elaine, she said, "Thank you. I still miss my brother, but for the first time since he died, I feel peace."

ଓ ଓଓ ଓ

Commentary on the Listening Questions

In the interest of giving proper credit, the Listening Questions in this chapter were partially influenced by five questions developed by Bruce Di Marsico in the 1960's, to which I have added several more. Many psychologists have adapted Bruce's five questions to their needs; but with very different purposes and goals than the purposes and goals shared here for biblical counsel. Questions are just tools, and tools can be used in many different ways.

Psychological counseling, for example, seeks to increase a person's sense of personal confidence and well-being, with a goal of self-determination and positive self-identity. Biblical counsel seeks to increase a person's awareness of sin and the sovereignty of God, with a goal of trusting dependency on God made possible only through Jesus Christ, by faith.

Psychology vs. Biblical Wisdom

Psychology's view of the nature of man—who we are, why we do what we do, and how we change—is diametrically opposed to the Bible's view of the same:

Psychology says we are basically good.
Biblical truth says we are basically sinners.[21]

Psychology says listen to our heart.
Biblical truth says the heart is deceitful and wicked.[22]

Psychology says we have the answers inside of us.
Biblical truth says Jesus Christ is the only answer.[23]

Psychology says our goal is happiness.
Biblical truth says our goal is holiness.[24]

Psychology says we need to love ourselves.
Biblical truth says we must die to ourselves.[25]

Psychology says to focus on what we need.
Biblical truth says trust God with our needs.[26]

Psychology depends on human knowledge.
Biblical truth depends on God's Word.[27]

Psychology does not include the authority of God.
Biblical truth rests on the authority of God.[28]

The list could go on and on, but suffice to say these are diametrically opposed foundational principles. That doesn't mean psychology is necessarily useless, but it is no substitute for God's truth.

> *The foolishness of God is wiser than men, and the weakness of God is stronger than men (1 Corinthians 1:25).*

଴ ഈ଴ ഈ

Chapter 10 ~ Homework

1. Write out a few of the Listening Questions that you think might be most helpful:

2. Partner with someone in your group and have them ask you the Listening Questions about a situation you are facing in your life. Then reverse roles. What did you notice? (If you are doing this study alone, ask yourself the questions.) Remember your goal isn't to figure out how to fix the situation, but to listen for what desire is being worshipped.

Chapter 10 ~ Prayer

Lord God,

I thank You that there is no condemnation in You, and that through Jesus, I have been set free from the law of sin and death (from Romans 8:1). Give me humility of spirit and keep me from pridefulness, that I might be made useful for Your purposes. When I feel inadequate or uncertain, remind me I am only an instrument in Your hands. When helping others, may I rely not on my own understanding (Proverbs 3:5), or on clever words and questions, but on You—for You alone soften hearts and open eyes, revealing what needs to be revealed. In the name of Jesus Christ, amen.

Journal

Write out a dialogue on the issue you chose for this study, asking yourself the Listening Questions.

11. Practical Discipleship

Being asked to help someone examine their heart biblically is a sacred privilege, but it doesn't require a degree in counseling, a host of memorized Bible verses, or perfect godliness. It does require these seven things:

1. Understanding of God's authority, righteousness, sovereignty, grace, mercy, and love (Exodus 20:3).
2. Belief in the inerrancy, sufficiency, infallibility, and inspiration of the Bible (2 Timothy 3:16).
3. An understanding of the Gospel and a personal faith in Jesus Christ as Lord and Savior, certain He is the only way to the Father (John 3:16; 14:6).
4. An understanding of heart idolatry (Ezekiel 14:3).
5. A desire to please God above all (2 Corinthians 5:9).
6. Experience identifying and confessing idols of one's own heart and confidence in God's faithfulness to bless those who "earnestly and diligently seek Him" (2 Corinthians 1:4, Hebrews 11:6).
7. A willingness to listen (Proverbs 18:13), speak the truth in love (2 Timothy 4:2), and pray (1 Thessalonians 5:17).

Notice "x-ray vision" is not on that list. Although it's easy to tell when someone is in idolatry, it is impossible to know *what specific idol* they are worshipping until the Holy Spirit reveals it. You can explain the concept of idolatry, ask questions, and help sort out conflicting desires and fears. You can describe some possibilities of what they *might* be worshipping—if they have asked for that advice—confess what you would be tempted to worship if you were in their shoes, pray with them in repentance, and rejoice in what God has shown them . . . but you can't tell them what their idols are. That should be a relief.

ఆ ఇ

"Out of the overflow of the heart, the mouth speaks (Luke 6:45)," so when someone is in idolatry, they will testify to it by their own words. Their conversation will always focus on the following three self-reflective things:

1) How much they are hurting,
2) Who or what they see as the cause of that hurt, and
3) How hard they are trying to respond effectively.

These can be depicted on the Idols Chart by drawing three "U-turn" arrows on the Self-pleasing side of the chart that head toward the heart, but bounce off the line above it, as if looking into a one-way mirror. Essentially, they are "stuck above the line" in idolatry.

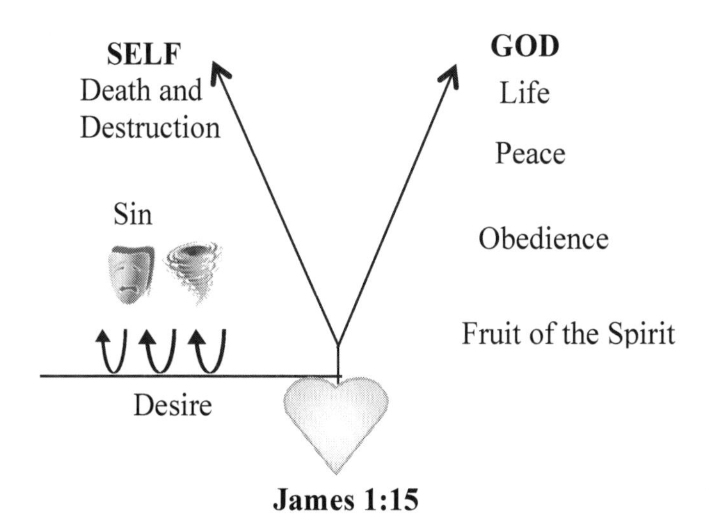

James 1:15

Desire when it has conceived gives birth to sin, and sin when it is full-grown, brings forth death.

cs so

A sense of hopelessness will surely be evident, and the problems presented so complicated and intractable, you may feel overwhelmed just listening to them. Remember that your goal is not to try to resolve those problems or even help that person achieve happiness. Your primary goal is to help them identify where they might be in wrong worship, confident God will move in their problems, once their heart is right.

Of course, you can and should give practical biblical advice for everyday situations. At the beginning, it may be just to give them hope as they experience the truth of God's Word. Later, it may help them learn more God-pleasing ways of handling things. Your primary concern at the start, however, is to carefully listen to their heart. It only takes a little idolatry to separate a person from the power and presence of God.

When the problem presented is a huge, complicated mess, assure the counselee (and yourself) of God's faithfulness in giving every person enough grace and strength for what they are facing (1 Corinthians 10:13). Rather than try to address everything at once, look for one small "thread" sticking out—some aspect of their situation in which you can help them apply God's truth.

For example, you could ask what led them to seek help at this particular time, or what upsetting thing happened most recently. You could role-play an upcoming worrisome interaction, or one that happened the day before. It doesn't really matter, because everything leads back to the heart. Correctly applying God's truth to one area of their life, works inward to change the heart, then outward to touch every aspect of their life. So, if the first thing you choose to work on doesn't seem to be going anywhere, look for another.

It feels a bit like following breadcrumbs through a forest, picking up and looking at each one as you go, curious where the trail might lead. Suddenly, you step out of the forest to find yourself at the foot of a giant temple, with the hurting person making sacrifices at the top and crying out in pain. Your job is to describe what you see, point them to the Christ, and explain the importance of worshipping God alone.

What happens next is up to God. If He opens their eyes, they will blink as if just wakened from a dream, perhaps weep with understanding, confess their heart, and praise Him. The temple will disappear, and you will be standing with that person in a beautiful clearing—the peace of God visibly evident on their face.

If their eyes aren't opened or they choose to shut them tight, nothing will happen. You can rest in knowing that "He who began a good work will bring it to completion at the day of Jesus Christ" (from Philippians 1:6). It may be that He just intended for you to plant seeds of truth to be harvested by someone else. Perhaps He wanted to remind you that it is He alone Who transforms hearts, not the skill of a counselor.

It is important to guard against having an idol of trying to get someone to see their idols or of trying to fix their situation. You will know when you are worshipping that idol by the lack of peace in your own heart, the urgent desire to Control for Success in your counseling, and the fear of failure.

> *Keep watch on yourself, lest you too be tempted (Galatians 6:1).*

☙ ❧

Conventional wisdom says it is best, even necessary, to meet with someone face-to-face when counseling. That may be true for psychologists; but God's ability to work in human hearts is not dependent on a person's ability to see your face. Meeting in person certainly has its advantages, but when it isn't possible or convenient, there is no reason to assume God will do less by other means. Paul himself testified to hearts being convicted through his letters:

> *Even though I made you grieve with my letter, I do not regret it—though I did regret it, for I see that that letter grieved you, though only for a little while.*

As it is, I rejoice, not because you were grieved, but because you were grieved into repenting. For you felt a godly grief, so that you suffered no loss through us. For godly grief produces a repentance that leads to salvation without regret, whereas worldly grief produces death (2 Corinthians 7:8-10).

There are even certain advantages to counseling in other ways than face to face. A telephone's lack of visual context, for example, gives a degree of anonymity that may make it easier for a person to be open and vulnerable early in the conversation. The enduring quality of email provides an opportunity for both counselee and counselor to read and reread what was shared.

These advantages, however, can also be disadvantages. Telephone conversations don't allow for body language, and emails don't allow for body language or vocal tone. The enduring quality of emails (and texts) is disadvantageous if something is misstated or misunderstood. Therefore, great care and extra time must be taken to express a generous measure of compassion and hope. Counseling by email is not by any means a shortcut.

Some people have found counseling by video chat very useful and it certainly offers some advantages. However, even though the counselee can see your face and vice versa, video chat lacks many of the physical cues and much of the personal connection of in-person communication, the anonymity of telephone calls, and enduring quality of phone or email. Plus, it has unique distractions of its own. Perhaps, as we use video chat more frequently in our daily lives, these disadvantages will become less important.

Personally, I prefer at least the first meeting to be in person, if at all possible, so that the counselee can see my concern and care. However, I counsel many people whom I have never met in person because of time or distance, and I've still seen God do marvelous works in their lives.

ꟹ ꟹ

When a marriage is in trouble, it is generally assumed both spouses need to be present for counseling, in order for meaningful change to take place. A complementarian view would seem to require it; and since each spouse tends to complain about the other's sins, establishing the truth of those complaints and addressing them would seem to necessitate it. It is almost certain *both* people in the marriage have a heart problem, and important matters like communication and intimacy require both people to participate.

However, it only takes one person turning away from the idols of their heart and back to God, for God's power to work in the marriage in miraculous ways. Not only is that person changed, but the one not participating in counseling is changed as well and the marriage blessed. I cannot overstate this enough, having seen it time and time again. God's ability to pour His grace and restoration over everything in a person's life when they are seeking Him cannot be overstated. It is unlike anything in traditional marriage counseling.

There are also significant advantages to counseling one spouse alone. Husbands and wives give such different descriptions of their marital problems, it's often hard to believe they are describing the same marriage. Since idols of the heart are best found in individual perceptions, it is very helpful to *not* have to spend time weighing each side's claims in order to establish a mutually agreed-upon narrative.

Furthermore, the need to protect one's idols is less strong when the other spouse is not present, making it easier to step into the vulnerability required for self-examination. Not having both people participating eliminates the irresistible temptation to focus on how to meet the other person's needs or get one's own needs met. It is easier to focus on God alone when no other option is available.

Loving correction and honest confrontation are much easier when you have only a person's own words to rely on for evidence. The simple statement, *"By your own words, you testified that ___________,"* is well received and responded to, when no one else has spoken; but it is often perceived as an attack or as taking sides, if the other spouse has previously commented on the subject.

Finally, there is an exceptional transformation of faith that takes place when a counselee sees God move and realizes His faithfulness depends on the condition of their own heart, not on someone else's willingness to seek Him.

There are of course equally compelling reasons for having both parties present and participating in the counseling, not the least of which is the opportunity for both to grow in faith. However, there is no reason to think God can do less in the marriage, when only one spouse is seeking counseling.

ଓ ଓ

Tess had been married for just six months, when she reached out to me through email. "My husband and I are both Bible college students and Bible Study leaders," she wrote, "but we are failing miserably in our marriage." She then described their situation, as well as her despair at finding out her husband had already contacted a lawyer:

> *My husband keeps track of all the things I've ever done wrong since we got married and holds them against me, even though I've apologized time and again, and asked his forgiveness. He ridicules and mocks me, using the very words of a counselor we once saw against me.*
>
> *Like a dictator, he bosses me, criticizing the smallest of things as not being done right. He even uses scripture against me sometimes, finding fault in everything I do. This morning he told me he had spoken to a lawyer about filing for divorce. I'm devastated.*

In my reply, I explained that as long as her heart was fixed on the wrong her husband was doing, she was probably worshipping the desire for him to change. God would not be in her efforts to restore the marriage, and even her prayers for her husband would go unheard. Although God might change her husband for His own reasons, she wouldn't reap the blessings of those changes. She probably wouldn't even see them.

"I'm not perfect," she said. "I lose my temper all the time and I know I shouldn't do that. But how do I get my husband to stop being so critical and controlling?"

"By your own words, you admitted just now that you can't control your own sin. How do you expect to control his?"

"But what am I supposed to do?"

"There is so much more to this than what you are seeing," I replied. "God is at work, challenging you and allowing you to be challenged, so that you will grow in holiness. Marriage is wonderful for revealing the sin in our hearts we didn't know we had. Put your focus on God, not what you need for happiness, and you will begin to see Him do amazing things."

"I'm just so afraid . . . and unhappy. I don't know how to let go of that."

I explained the concept of idols of the heart, then added: "God already knows your heart, so be honest with Him. Pray and tell Him where you are struggling and ask Him to reveal whatever idols you have in your heart regarding your husband. Set your heart on God rather than on what you need or want, and He will give you peace."

I didn't promise Tess that God would restore their marriage because the Bible doesn't say He will. I did, however, assure her of God's faithfulness and shared my confidence that if she set her heart on Him alone, He would bless her. "I can't say exactly what that will look like," I wrote. "God might change your husband or He might change you so that what used to upset you no longer bothers you. Whatever He does, however, I know it will be a blessing to you."

Tess replied a few days later, saying she was certain she had made wanting her husband to be more loving an idol—which had led her to become increasingly manipulative, nagging, angry, critical, self-pitying, and self-righteous.

Whenever he did something that gave her hope for change, she was happy. Whenever he returned to his old ways, she was angry and miserable.

"I imagine God probably desires your husband to be godly and loving more than you do," I wrote. "However, by making sacrifices and offerings to try to bring that about, you have been worshipping those desires, rather than God."

Tess confessed and repented, and God immediately began softening her heart for her husband *and her husband's heart for her.* She was amazed, since she had not shared with her husband anything she had learned, and he was not getting counsel or advice from anyone else.

Three days later, her husband told her he had changed his mind about the divorce, saying he considered their marriage "something to be cherished as one of the most important things in their lives." It was a dramatic turnaround for a man who had seen a lawyer just one week earlier. When Tess wrote to tell me the good news, it was not with self-serving celebration for those changes, but with humility and submission to God.

> *It is amazing how much things have changed in our marriage, but more importantly in my faith. For months I felt sorry for myself and for what my life had become, looking only at myself and my circumstances. I am so thankful that God has shown me how I was dishonoring Him. I want none of that destructive worldly sorrow to occupy my heart any longer. The only sorrow I desire now is the sorrow that comes from seeing where I have sinned. That sorrow I can take to God and be cleansed.*

After a while, Tess slipped back into her old ways—as we all tend to do when things are going well. Her next email was like the first, with another long list of the hurtful things her husband was doing, a description of how miserable she was, and complaints of how hard she had tried to respond in a God-pleasing way. I was glad to see in the end, however, that she looked on her lack of God's peace as evidence of how serious He was about the condition of her heart.

Once again, Tess repented, and once again God began moving in her marriage. Things that had previously sent her into a rage no longer upset her. Her husband expressed remorse about his failings as a husband, asked her forgiveness, and began to seek discipleship and wisdom from godly men. Six months later she sent this update:

> *It has been so much better from six months ago. My husband has become a wonderful prayer warrior. He was recently asked to help in children's ministry and our home atmosphere every night has been blessed as he reads and prepares for that. Together we are participating in Bible study.*
>
> *I confess I still struggle with my "God-replacement" desires, however. Not so much in my marriage (praise God!) but in adjusting to this new role as a wife, living in a new city, wishing this or that . . . which inadvertently affects how I treat my husband. I realize now, all of that was masquerading as "marriage problems" when I first wrote you that we were doing deplorably bad. God has done so much in us—I know He will continue to do more!*

Tess was right: God *was* going to do more. Just after that email, they went through another difficult period; but this time she didn't slip back into her former self-pitying heart and fixation on his wrongdoing. Instead, she asked God what He was trying to show her—and do in her—through those challenges. She was coming to appreciate that growing in godliness was not just a matter of fixing a few things and being done, or even getting a Bible college degree. It was a life-long process that would consistently be the most challenging, enriching, and rewarding experience she would ever have. Some weeks later she wrote:

> *We've just come through one and a half months of serious struggles and more threats of separation, but in a strange way it has helped me understand more. My mind is cleared as the Lord broke me free from my former sense of entitlement—the idea that I deserve a good life because I love God.*
>
> *I realized I was depending on good things that had happened as evidence of having "arrived" in my faith. But every time I start counting on my own strength, the good things that were happening were stripped away. God is showing me I have to rely totally on Him. He has proven He can rebuild our marriage. Why do I keep trying to make things happen as if I were better than God?*

You can clearly hear the changes taking place in Tess' heart, in particular the way she was becoming much more aware of her own sin and focused on what God is doing in her, than on her husband's sin and what she wanted God to do in him. The regret she expressed wasn't the self-condemning guilt that is so contrary to the Gospel, but true conviction that comes from the Holy Spirit. Tess was truly learning to walk in Christ, live her faith in every aspect of her life, and enjoy the blessings of doing so. Exactly one year after we first began corresponding, she sent this observation:

> *Through this experience, I've come to realize the consequences of my own sins, and how much I contribute to our difficulties. I no longer feel paralyzed by guilt or anger when I know I am not doing what I should. I am resting in God's plan, certain He knows the gap between my knowledge/faith and how I apply/live it. I am a work in progress; and He is a gracious God, who pardons us, without condemnation.*
>
> *He has shown me so many things in regard to my own call as a wife I didn't know before, things I couldn't see about myself. The amazing thing is that He has done so* through *this marriage: without it, I would not have understood. It was through our difficulties He revealed them to me.*
>
> *Today, I look at everything through the lens of what God is doing in me, rather than what I want Him to do in my husband—or anyone else for that matter—and I am so grateful for this new way of living out my faith. Seeking to please God is no longer something I just want to do. It's become a way of life that's transformed my faith. Praise Him.*

I rejoiced to see Tess was no longer thinking of marriage as a place to find happiness, but as a living, dynamic stage on which God was constantly molding and shaping her in the image of Christ. Not long after that email, Tess became pregnant; and nine months later she wrote to express her and her husband's joy over their beautiful baby daughter.

☙ ❧

The conflict of interest inherent in trying to identify a desire, in order to ask God to take it away, makes it difficult to see one's own heart accurately. "The heart is deceitful above all things, and desperately sick; who can understand it?" (Jeremiah 29:11). Pride is always involved in some way or another, but other things might add to that difficulty.

An **unbeliever**, for example, may intellectually understand idolatry and even recognize a potential idol of their heart. However, the significance of idolatry as sinful worship will be lost on them, without the conviction of the Holy Spirit.

Someone who has spent years in the study of **psychology** or received lengthy psychological counseling may tend to speak psychologically. This often leads to a habit of trying to reframe or restate concepts—even God's Truth—in psychological terms. This is both an intellectual distraction and an error of logic. Essentially, it treats psychology as the standard of truth against which biblical truth should be weighed and removes God from both the problem and the solution.

Someone who is taking **anti-depressants** may draw near enough to their heart to see an idol and identify it, but then bounce gently off and away from the surface of their heart as though an invisible shield were protecting it. That's not surprising, given the nature of anti-depressants; but it does make it difficult to feel the deep conviction necessary for the relinquishment of an idol. *Never suggest a person make changes in their medication if you are not their physician, and do not make changes to your own medication without consulting your physician.*

Someone with a **prideful, defensive spirit**, or who is engaged in **willful sin**, will very likely resist the *suggestion* of idolatry—even more, the idea of confessing one. Ironically, someone with a **humble spirit** may have a similar challenge, if they're accustomed to burying painful feelings—which is not uncommon if they or their spouse have been serving in the church for many years. They may feel that examining their heart for idols would be like opening a Pandora's box[29] of past issues that would be better (or safer) left alone.

People-pleasers may rush to identify and confess their idols so quickly that they miss the point entirely. Conversely, people who ***surround*** **themselves with people-pleasers** may have so few opportunities for idols to be frustrated or exposed, that they find it difficult to imagine they have any idols at all.

Finally, **Bible study teachers**—myself included—may have more difficulty seeing and confessing our idols than even new believers. First, we have become so adept at speaking in godly-sounding terms that we inadvertently justify or cloak our idols in supposed righteousness. Second, there is often pride involved in not wanting to be guilty of sin. Third, our love for intellectual mastery makes us resistant to surrendering ourselves fully to God until we have everything figured out—as you saw in my testimony at the end of Chapter 9.

We also like to organize concepts in neat, organized boxes or twelve-week lesson plans to be mastered and taught. Arming ourselves with knowledge, we slip into thinking we can keep sin at bay without dying to ourselves—sometimes losing touch with the sweet vulnerability of complete dependency on God. My friend Christine Russell, a Bible study leader whom I've been blessed to mentor on idols of the heart for several years, testifies to this beautifully:

> *We can study the scriptures diligently and yet end up missing Him, and I find myself so easily tripped up in that regard—resisting the call to trust God alone. As women in ministry, we resist the vulnerability that requires, and try instead to serve Him from a position of growing knowledge, willpower, and spiritual strength. But it's in the vulnerability of relinquishing all our desires that we come to understand Who He is.*

Fortunately, God's Word is "sharper than any two-edged sword, piercing to the division of soul and of spirit, of joints and of marrow, and discerning the thoughts and intensions of the heart" (Hebrews 4:12). Surely it can pierce through psychology, medications, pride, defensiveness, comfortable humility, and even intellectual self-sufficiency to set us all free. All we have to do is ask (Matthew 7:7).

☙ ❧

Sometimes, I am so eager for a hurting person to experience God's peace that I come across as abrupt or even self-righteous. I pray continually for a spirit of gentleness, that I might be "completely humble and gentle, patient and bearing with one another in love"—giving reason for my hope with gentleness and respect (Ephesians 4:2, 1 Peter 3:15). Perhaps you have the opposite challenge of hesitant shyness. If so, you can pray for a spirit of boldness according to 2 Corinthians 3:12, which says, *"Since we have such a hope, we are bold."*

We can each thank God for our own daily struggles with idolatry, as painful as they may be, because it is by and through those struggles that He gives us the confident boldness *and* compassionate understanding we need to help others . . . and a not-so-gentle reminder that His work in us is not yet finished (Philippians 1:6).

Knowing how to discern our idols and help others do the same doesn't exempt us from struggling with idolatry ourselves. Nor does it prevent us from being tempted to rage, when those idolatrous desires are threatened. It does help us to recognize more quickly when we are in idolatry. Having seen and experienced His faithfulness when idols are confessed gives us greater courage and confidence to confess our own. It also makes us more accountable to do so.

> *Everyone to whom much was given, of him much will be required (Luke 12:48).*

ꕥ ꕥ

Chapter 11 ~ Homework

1. What things are necessary in order to help someone examine their heart biblically? Which of these do you feel are your strongest or weakest points?

2. What are some of the things that make it hard for people to see their own hearts accurately? Which might apply to you?

Chapter 11 - Prayer

Lord God,

I praise You and bless You. I confess my heart is given to idolatry. Increase my faith (Luke 17:5) and give me the desire to worship only You. Take my eyes off of whatever or whomever I accuse as the source of my difficulty, and expose the sin in my own heart (Mark 4:22). Take away my prideful self-defense and give me a humble and vulnerable spirit. Pour out Your light into the dark and hidden places of my heart. Give me eyes to see, ears to hear (Mark 4:23), and a mind to understand whatever it is You want me to know, in order that I might walk in Your truth for life. I submit all my desires to You today, oh Lord, by the power of Your Holy Spirit and in the name of Jesus Christ. Amen.

Journal

The greatest temptation when reading this book is to create a new idol in the heart of "not having any idols." Explain the theological difference between seeking to obey the Lord vs. trying to perfect your own heart. From a practical standpoint, is the difference mostly behavioral or motivational? How does the Gospel fit in? How is Romans 7:24-25 a message of hope?

12. Changed Hearts

There once was a marriage so terrible, I trembled to discuss the concepts in this book with the young woman who shared her struggle with our small group. Her husband, a professed believer, had physically abused her two years previously, but that had stopped when she involved the police and her in-laws. Recently, however, he had become increasingly moody and angry, and he still engaged in forms of emotional and economic abuse. After a dozen difficult years, Arianna was exhausted from trying to please God without seeing much, if any, change.

Had I not known how deeply idolatry separates a person from God's wisdom and peace and favor in *all* circumstances, I would have been tempted to give her one recommendation in the flesh: leave and leave quickly. Helping her examine her heart for areas of wrong worship, instead, turned out to be a profound and life-changing experience.

Let me say first that this story is not shared with a spirit of condemnation for those who have ended an abusive marriage. True, God hates divorce, but staying married doesn't earn anyone a ticket to heaven. It is shared simply to give encouragement and hope to those who are struggling to trust God in seemingly impossible situations.

If reading it causes you any feelings of regret, guilt, or shame for the past, remember that Jesus never dwelt on the past. Resist the devil's temptations to do so, yourself. Set your heart fully on God today and move forward in as God-pleasing a manner as possible. God won't just forget the past as though it never happened, He will turn it around and use it for His glory and your blessing.

> *Forgetting what lies behind and straining forward to what lies ahead, I press on toward the goal for the prize of the upward call of God in Christ Jesus (from Philippians 3:13).*

Arianna's Testimony

"Arianna," I said, after she finished telling the group of her struggle, "you are blessed to live in a country where it is illegal to abuse a wife or children, and there are places where you can go for protection. If you feel your husband is becoming abusive again, or fear you or the children are in any danger, you should notify the authorities and go somewhere safe. You can still examine your heart for idols and pray for your husband from there."

She assured the group she wouldn't hesitate to call the police or leave the house if she felt she or the children were in danger. Her faith was strong from a decade of earnestly praying for her husband and leaning on the Lord for solace and comfort, but she was weary and hurting.

"I just want to know why God isn't answering my prayers," she said.

I began by saying honestly, "I don't know that if I were in your shoes, I could believe or act on what I am going to share with you. But I know God gives grace enough for every situation, and I know God is faithful . . ."

She nodded. "I believe that."

" . . . And I know that if you find some area of your heart that is not aligned with God and realign it with Him, He will do something. I don't know what, specifically, He will do. It will probably be surprising; it will probably happen quickly; and it will probably be something that seems insignificant to others, but is deeply significant to you. If you're interested in walking that journey of faith, I'm willing to walk it with you if you want me to."

"I am, and I do," Arianna said. "But will God change my husband?"

"I don't know. He will certainly change you. He might change your husband. He might allow your husband to remove himself from your life. He might even take his life as He took Nabal's life in the Bible (1 Samuel 25:3)."

"I don't want God to take my husband's life!"

"I'm not saying He will; but He always moves on behalf of those who wait on Him and are called according to His purpose (Isaiah 64:4, Romans 8:28).

"Psalm 31:19 is one of my favorite verses," Arianna said. "'How abundant are the good things You have stored up for those who fear You, that You bestow in the sight of all on those who take refuge in You.' She smiled."

"Exactly."

We talked through some of the Listening Questions, and Arianna soon identified an idol in her heart of wanting her husband to change. As soon as she asked God to remove that desire as an idol, she felt His comfort and peace. Then as a group, we discussed some of the practical ways a wife in a difficult marriage could honor God without falling into the temptation of becoming a martyr or a doormat.[30]

"Whatever you do, no matter *what* you do," I concluded, "do it all to the glory of God, giving thanks to God through Christ (1 Corinthians 10:31, Colossians 3:17). No eye has seen, no hear has heard, no heart has imagined, what God has prepared for those who love him (1 Corinthians 2:9)."

The next week, Arianna shared several amazing things God had done in her, in their marriage, *and* in her husband. The second and third weeks, she added to that testimony. The fourth week, however, she told us her husband had come to her in their bedroom one evening and abusively pushed himself on her physically and sexually. Then he had stood glaring at her in the doorway, his eyes burning with anger and hatred, saying the devil had sent him to torment her.

"Arianna . . .," I interrupted, with grave concern.

"He has pushed himself on me before," she said. "In the past, it left me emotionally numb for days. This time, though, I had unexplainable peace. The next day, he apologized and when he asked why I wasn't angry, I told him I didn't know . . . I just wasn't. I was filled with God's love for him, and forgiveness. It was something I tried to have. God *gave* me His love for my husband. When I told him that, He put his head down and said he knew it was God and asked me to pray for him."

Two weeks later, Arianna testified that their marriage was growing in tenderness and love. She said the hateful incident had tested her heart and given her confidence her motives were rooted in pleasing God. It had also given her firm assurance God was with her and more powerful than anything anyone could do to her. Then she said she believed God wanted her to start giving her paychecks to her husband to let him manage the family finances.

I was taken aback and uncomfortable with the idea. She had previously told the group her husband spent his own paychecks unwisely, requiring her to provide for all the family's needs through the small salary she made. Concerned she was trying to rush things in her own strength, I said, "There is certainly biblical support for letting your husband manage the money, but I confess it makes me nervous. My mind is spinning with all the 'what ifs' that could happen."

"Me too," she said honestly. "But I am completely at peace about it."

"Peace can come from many sources; but it is not my place to try to turn you from what you feel God desires you to do, as long as it is not contrary to His Word. Just make sure your motive is to please God, without regard for the result."

"I have," she said, "and I trust this is what God desires me to do, no matter what happens."

Arianna's weekly testimonies of the changes God was working in both her and her husband continued to amaze us. She was becoming more and more sensitive to the subtle ways her heart engaged in and led her to sin; and her husband was becoming more loving, financially responsible, and generous. He was also exhibiting greater tenderness toward her and the children. Although he sometimes still struggled with his temper, he never again behaved maliciously.

As the weeks went by, a surprising thing began to happen: Arianna began to doubt her faith. Having clung to God in heartache for so long, she wasn't sure what a relationship with God looked like when things were going well. She even began to wonder if she was saved, as the fire of desperate faith that had sustained her all those years became a warmer, softer glow of peace. Gradually, those concerns about her salvation faded, but she was surprised how much harder it was to feel close to God when she wasn't desperate for Him.

Six months later, God was still blessing and moving in Arianna's marriage. Her husband had not yet come to a saving faith in Jesus; but in a way that made the transformation God was doing in his heart in such a short period of time even more astounding. One by one his sinful behaviors—and hers—were dropping away, and they were learning to express the kind of loving-kindness God commands of husbands and wives.

Four years after she first wrote, I emailed Arianna to check on her and ask how they were doing. She replied:

> *It is truly amazing how my husband loves me so much, now! He appreciates me, honors me, sacrifices himself for me, and leads our little family with love . . . and I have done nothing other than discipline my heart away from idolatry and honor my husband through the Lord!*
>
> *There's a depth to our marriage, now, that is beautiful. My husband is growing as a loving and self-sacrificing leader, and I am growing in learning how to make room in my heart for God to lead him in that way. Sometimes I do slip up, but*

as I remind myself of God's faithfulness and repent of my own sin, God begins to move again and bless us in ways more beautiful than before.

My husband is growing in his faith, and our relationship keeps growing in richness. Our children are benefiting, too. And our home—which used to be just a place where we happened to live—is peaceful now.

I feel like God has taken away my old, hateful and abusive husband and given me a new, godly one, the way He took Nabal's life and gave Abigail a new husband in David.[31] *Only He made him a new husband . . . and me a new wife.*

I didn't think people could change, and certainly not as much as we have, but God has taken an angry, abusive man, and turned him into a loving, tenderhearted one. He has changed me from a woman of desperation and idolatry into one who knows and trusts the Lord in all things.

Who else but God could have worked such sudden and lasting changes, giving her earthly happiness and the eternal joy that comes from witnessing His power? No human wisdom, no amount of psychology could have brought about such a thing.

Staying in a difficult marriage didn't make Arianna more righteous than leaving it; but it did enable her to experience God move in profound and dramatic ways. She no longer thought of her marriage as a burden to bear in order to please God, but as the very means by which God was revealing Himself to her and blessing her.

Just recently, I checked in with Arianna again—eight years after we met. She writes:

> *Years ago my path with my husband could have easily ended in destruction, but we persisted; and I am so thankful, because every day we are living God's blessing. Even though the past was pretty terrible at times, I wouldn't change it. We didn't give up, and now it is all part of our beautiful story and a praise to God's glory.*
>
> *My journey with you in learning to honor God in my life helped my husband to be raised up and be led away from the dysfunction and filth of his childhood, which was all he knew and had carried into our home. I rejoiced over each small, miraculous step forward. Although the improvements were day by day, it all happened so rapidly I can only explain it as seeing God move mountains that I truly thought could never be moved.*
>
> *Our two lovely daughters are now young teens, and we have a "surprise" little boy, a year and a half old. My husband's love for our son has changed him as a farther and brought healing to his relationship with our daughters, as well as with his own mother (who would have thought!) as he now understands the love she has for him. He is a completely different person, gentle and loving—the best husband and father we could ever hope for, pouring everything into guiding and strengthening our kids. God is so good.*

ᘛ ᘚ

Carmen's Testimony

Carmen's marriage wasn't difficult, but it was joyless and short on love—from her side. We had become friends, just as she was finishing up the course work for a doctoral program in geology, and occasionally met to talk about things of God. At first she was quite skeptical about the concept of idols of the heart; but as she applied them to her life and experienced God's faithfulness, she was eager to know more. We stayed in touch after my husband and I returned to the USA, and I loved hearing how God was filling their marriage with love and joy.

One day, Carmen wrote in a panic to say her husband wanted to move back to Venezuela in order to be closer to their families. The idea of leaving a land of freedom and blessing for one of oppression and poverty did not please Carmen at all. She was sure it was not in the children's best interest and was having trouble trusting God or believing He would work everything out for good:

> *I am praying for God to give me a heart that trusts Him and wisdom to know what to do on a day-by-day basis. I know I don't really trust God. I guess that is a good start. I know my prayers have been double-minded and I recognize that before God.*
>
> *I had been feeling so confident because now I know how to search my heart for idols. I was amazed at what God did when I relinquished one just two*

> *weeks ago. Now I feel like I'm stuck again because I don't want to relinquish this one. It is almost like a spiritual tongue-twister: I feel like because I know I don't trust in Him fully, I can't do anything other than trust that He will help me trust in Him.*

I love that last sentence: *"I feel like because I know I don't trust in Him fully, I can't do anything other than trust that He will help me trust in Him.*" Such complete dependence on God is exactly what He desires. We tend to submit to Him as a last resort, only after all our own efforts have been exhausted; but He calls us to submit our hearts to Him from the start, even when it seems to lead away from what we think is best.

Carmen's husband persisted with the idea of moving, and soon they were relocated to a small, two-bedroom house near his aging parents in a country on the verge of economic collapse. His sister moved in with them—"just until she could get on her feet," he had said—and Carmen found herself sharing one bedroom with her daughter and the sister-in-law, while her husband shared a second bedroom with their son.

Jealousy regarding her husband's sense of obligation to his family soon rose up in Carmen's heart, along with resentment over the sleeping arrangements and responsibilities of caring for an additional person. She longed to visit her own parents, hours away, but the money she had set aside to do so had been spent on car repairs and settling into the new house.

Then there were concerns about the children's quality of education and lack of exposure to the world. To make matters worse, Carmen had to deal with subtle family and cultural pressures to drop her doctoral aspirations and accept a more traditional role. It was hard to concentrate on finishing her doctoral dissertation in such an environment.

I could hear in Carmen's emails how much she desired to please God; but it sounded like her motivation was primarily in order to get Him to "fix things." So, I encouraged her to check her heart by asking herself the following question:

> **Am I seeking to please God with all I have today, or seeking to please God to get what I want tomorrow?**

The following day, Carmen wrote:

> *I was quite upset and angry yesterday. However, as I started working through the Listening Questions, writing down what I think I need in order to be happy and what I am afraid of, I could feel my heart soften and grow peaceful. I realized that sometimes when I say I am obeying God, it is out of a heart that thinks/hopes He will then give me what I want—to get whatever "blessings" I want from Him rather than a desire to serve Him. Romans 6:16 came to mind, about being a slave to obedience, rather than to sin.*
>
> *But that just made me realize how many idols I had and wonder, "How do I get rid of them all?" God has been ripping away my "safety nets" one by one—all the escape hatches I had in place in case trusting God didn't work out how I thought it should. I had been thinking of my faith as a journey in the desert that would come to an end, if I had enough faith.*

Later, I read Hebrews 1:13, which says, "All these people were still living by faith when they died. They did not receive the things promised," and I realized faith is independent of results on this earth. God softened my heart and showed me so much through those verses. I had never looked so deeply into my heart before. It feels like I've discovered a new door to a hidden, dusty old closet. There's a lot of cleaning that needs to take place, but strangely, I feel so much peace!

How exciting it was to see Carmen focusing less on her circumstances, and more on whether or not she was pleasing God in her response to those circumstances. I especially loved her observation that faith is "independent of results on this earth." At the end of that email, she added:

You know, it really unsettled me when you first wrote, "Ask yourself how you can seek to please God in your life as it is today; rather than how you can please Him to get what you want tomorrow." It was exactly what I didn't want to hear. Only when I started focusing on what God wanted from me more than what I wanted from Him did His plan begin to unfold. Only then could I see how much better His plan was than mine.

Learning to stop focusing on my circumstances and hold to the truth that God is truly trustworthy and knows what is best for me, has been the single most significant faith lesson of my life.

12. Changed Hearts

Over the next year, Carmen continued to turn her heart toward God, and He did many wonderful things—in her own heart as well as in the hearts of those around her. Her sister-in-law began helping with the children and housework, giving Carmen time to finally complete her dissertation. Carmen's husband found creative ways for the two of them to spend time alone in marital intimacy, and their marriage grew to a level of warmth and closeness that was deeper and richer than anything they had known before.

Carmen was amazed. "I loved my husband before," she wrote. "But it was more like I chose to love him. Now I feel deep, godly love for my husband." Soon, she and her husband were expecting their third child. During the pregnancy, Carmen wrote with frustration about a particular situation she was having trouble resolving in her heart:

> *There is a big shortage at the moment with basic products, and long lines everywhere to get everything. Today I went to the pharmacy for something I would need after my daughter's birth, but there was quite a line outside. When I saw it, my heart shook.*
>
> *Back home I cried. "Why do I have to live like this?" I thought. "Why do we have to live here?" Recognizing there was pride in my humiliation at the prospect of having to stand in line for three hours for something so necessary, I asked God to humble my heart and give me strength. Then, I asked Him to help me accept my husband's point of view that we*

were supposed to be living here, stop blaming him for bringing us here, and stop thinking him stubborn for keeping us here.

God led me to read 2 Corinthians 4:5 about being a servant for love, to Christ—which made me think of being a servant to my husband. Verse 7 described exactly how I felt that day: a clay pot, nothing else. Verse 15 talked about suffering for love, which made me think about being willing to suffer for love . . . to my husband, to my parents, to my children, to God.

And verses 17 and 18, wow . . . no need to say anything about those: "For this light momentary affliction is preparing for us an eternal weight of glory beyond all comparison, as we look not to the things that are seen but to the things that are unseen. For the things that are seen are transient, but the things that are unseen are eternal."

Later, I tried asking myself the Idols Test statements and Listening Questions: "What do I need to feel happy?" and "What am I afraid might happen?" But I couldn't find a straight answer no matter how hard I tried.

I knew that if I was sure I could find all the products I needed, I would feel better. But the truth is, I have all I need for today and I won't need those items until the baby comes. I just want the security of knowing I will have it later.

Then there is the issue that every time I read bad news or face the country's reality, I feel some resentment toward my husband again for bringing us here and not thinking of our children's future.

So I am wondering if maybe the idol of my heart is wanting my husband to react or respond differently and be more open about leaving the country? But on the other hand, I don't necessarily wish we would leave, as it would be hard for me to leave my family behind. I am so confused!

Normally, I would have responded right away with words of encouragement, but I didn't see her email for several days. By then, God had shown her all she needed to know:

All day Tuesday I checked my email every hour hoping you would respond. I was frightened by the idea of not being able to figure out my idols. I even doubted I was a child of God at all. I felt so little, so unable.

During the Christmas holidays I had had such a peace about being here in this country, and became convinced it was God's will. I was wondering how all that peace could fade away in just a few weeks. I thought maybe it was not real. Maybe I had just faked it because I was happy.

Wednesday I woke up with a "downcast face." It was pretty clear to me I had an idol in my heart, but I didn't want to think about it. I didn't want to give God my desire of economic security, of being able to provide for my children, of having some significance in life. Suddenly, it all came together. I was so afraid of the future. I pictured myself like Rachel, sitting on my hidden idols.

That night, before going to bed I wrote: "After all I have studied to earn my doctorate, after all my effort, here I am a woman without a job, depending on a man who is full of fears and insecurities, in a country that is sinking . . .."

Then, Thursday, I woke up feeling peace, though I can't explai[illegible]. We had a wonderful day and my heart was softened, so I prayed: "Dear God, I am sorry, I thank You for all You are and do in my life day after day. If things don't change and I have to find out how to substitute for the things I need, I'll do it. Thank You for my husband, help me love him and serve him. In Jesus Name, Amen."

I felt delight in thinking about who God is and I started praising Him. Then, I remembered I could still ask God for what I needed, so I prayed: "Dear God, You know once the baby comes I will need those things. Help me trust that You will provide for all my needs at the right time, Amen."

A few weeks later, Carmen shared a situation where she submitted to God rather than sink into bitterness and self-pity. You can easily hear how God is continuing to transform her heart and conform it to His—and how she is delighting in having Him do so.

Yesterday, my sister-in-law called to ask my husband for some money to pay for a battery for her car. It bothers me when she calls at the last minute, asking him to do things without first asking if he can or if he is busy. So, I was immediately in a bad mood.

Buying a car battery in my country is a complicated issue these days, involving waiting in lines for fifteen hours or more. As she works and is not able to do that, she paid someone to stand in line for her. It's a common thing to do, but my husband was worried they might deceive her by saying they stood in line then give her a cleaned-up old battery and take her money. So, he wanted to go with her to meet the guy and install the battery.

I asked him if it was that complicated. "Can't she just change and plug the thing in herself?" He said it wasn't easy and he felt he needed to help.

We went to the bank and while he stood in line to get money from the cash machine, I waited inside in the aircon. Alone, I started complaining to God, telling Him I didn't want to do this, asking why we always have to do things for his sister, complaining that she is so dependent on my husband, and so on

I felt like God then said: "It is My will for you to help her unconditionally, not for who she is, but because I command you. You would like to have a helping hand if you were alone; and I don't love you or care for you because of who you are or what you have done, but because it is My will."

So I prayed: "God help me do this with a pure heart, not with a resentful one or because I am afraid of what my husband could say, but for You." As I prayed, I felt my heart soften, and God gave me the grace to be there with my husband with a pure heart.

That is nothing to boast about, as my will was not good and I did not have the strength to obey. So, I can only boast on Him for strengthening me. It was such a little thing, yet so important to me.

This morning my husband told me he also struggles at times with how much his sisters lean on him. In the past, I would have felt happy about that kind of comment, as if it gave me the right to not want to help them. But this time I took the opportunity to share my heart with him and tell him what God had done in my heart. He told me he was so thankful for my patience and love.

Lately, I'm beginning to realize how self-righteous I feel about many things: judging others, trying to "help" those who are "not as godly" as I am. I realize how little, how weak, how dependent I am on God. I still have fears, so I pray He will set me free from the fear of suffering in this life.

I also recognize I don't fully thank God for His grace or consider it sufficient to me. I am still complaining to Him even about the possibility of suffering. So, I am praying for God to help me value what He provides and embrace living for Him.

I am so happy about my growing relationship with the Lord. Being able to see my heart in everyday things, and know how to call on God for help gives me such a sense of my dependency on Him and of the bigness of His grace.

As I was updating this chapter, I wrote Carmen to ask how she was doing, given that news from her country showing long bread lines and empty store shelves. She replied:

> *It is hard here, with babies and little children spending days and days lining up for food. There is so much suffering and struggling. Yet, God has been so good and merciful with us. However the situation is getting more and more difficult, so I just ask Him to help me trust in Him, no matter what, to take my fears away and to trust He is my provider.*
>
> *I thank God for this time here in our country, because it has helped me grow in ways I think I would never, ever have grown in the comfort of Australia. I know now how to live in abundance, because I am learning to live in scarcity with joy and peace, even more than before.*
>
> *In fact, I feel I still have abundance in every way possible! I know our country is in God's hands and in God's heart; and He is building a new nation, one that can give Him the glory.*

I shared so much of Carmen's correspondence to show that learning to examine your heart for idols and seeking to please God are not singular events. We don't just repent of an idol—even our biggest idol—and never have idolatry again. Learning to examine your heart accurately is a life-long journey of faith, one where every difficult situation or temptation becomes an opportunity to grow in Christ and experience God's grace and freedom.

Carmen marveled recently how eight years ago, she was absolutely certain the best thing for her family was *not* to return to their native country. Now, she is grateful for returning, for it is through her experiences there she has come to truly know the joy of the Lord.

> *Indeed, I count everything as loss because of the surpassing worth of knowing Christ Jesus my Lord (Philippians 3:8).*

ᏅᏘᏅᏘ

Chapter 12 - Homework

1. Looking back on the lifeline you created in your Journal at the beginning of this study, identify the events that have had the greatest impact on your faith. Is there a common thread?

2. What idols of the heart, might you find yourself dealing with, related to key events or situations in your life?

3. Was there anything in Arianna's or Carmen's stories that resonated with your own?

Chapter 12 - Prayer

Lord God,

I thank You for what You are doing in my life, especially in revealing my idolatries and helping me discern them so that I might love You wholeheartedly and submit myself to You. May I have a gentle and humble heart as I listen to others who are hurting, and may I delight in sharing Your Word. Let me not become so overwhelmed by the pain or circumstances of others that I become fearful, forgetting You always give rest to the weary (Matthew 11:28-30). May I be filled with all joy and peace in believing, so that by the power of Your Holy Spirit I abound in hope (Romans 15:13), in the name of Jesus Christ, amen.

Journal

How has your experience with the issue you chose to explore for this study enabled you to help others?

13. A Matter of Faith

The desires and fears that run through our minds and hearts form a large part of what we might call our "self-identity"—the "just who I am" of who we think we are. Relinquishing them requires a type of dying to Self, which isn't possible without the new life and new identity found in Christ's love. Any discussion of idolatry, therefore, will of necessity include a discussion of the Gospel.

Never presume someone's faith. I've heard men and women give amazing testimonies of God's miraculous provision or protection, without once testifying to His provision of a Savior. I even once met a pastor's wife who confessed she was able to keep her lack of faith a secret for a decade, because everyone assumed she believed; and many people today call themselves a Christian or a believer without having the slightest idea what either term really means. A Christian isn't just someone who tries to live and love like Christ; and a believer isn't someone who just believes in God.

Currently, my favorite way to learn about a person's faith is to ask: *"Who is Jesus to you, personally?"* Since most of the people I speak to are church-going Christians, it might be surprising to learn only 10% clearly and confidently answer, "He is my Lord and Savior."

These I call **Full Believers** because they tend to be as confident of God's righteousness as they are of His love (Jeremiah 9:24). Neither considering sin lightly, nor becoming paralyzed by self-condemnation, they know "where sin increases, grace abounds all the more" (Romans 5:20), and they acknowledge it is impossible to fully understand God's love without understanding His judgment of sin. Such people generally welcome a discussion of idols of the heart as a helpful and practical application of the Gospel—one that increases their ability to see their sin more clearly and enjoy God's grace more fully.

On the opposite side of the spectrum are **Non-Believing Believers.** These are people who self-identify as Christians and believe in God, but give very vague and evasive answers when asked about Jesus. They may be able to identify an idol, but without the Holy Spirit they are not moved to conviction, much less true repentance. An explanation of the nature of idolatry is a wonderful doorway to sharing the Gospel with them.

Between these two extremes are Love Believers and Righteousness Believers. **Love Believers** have a faith focused on God's righteousness as expressed in His love and grace, but are uncomfortable with God's righteousness as expressed in His judgment of sin. They tend to respond to the question, "Who is Jesus to you?" with things like, "*I love Jesus. He's very important to me,*" "*He is love,*" or, "*He is Lord*"—while carefully avoiding any mention of sin or the need for salvation. Deeply concerned with not judging others, Love Believers can end up with a weak or undiscerning faith—one where everyone is viewed as equally good rather than equally sinful. Generally responding well to teaching on idolatry, they find in it a new understanding of sin and appreciation for the Gospel.

Righteousness Believers have a faith that is, in a sense, the doctrinal opposite of Love Believers: full of understanding of God's righteousness as expressed in His judgment of sin, but lacking understanding of His righteousness as expressed in His grace and love. Even when they believe in Jesus as their Savior, they tend to give works-based answers about salvation and/or sanctification. Righteousness Believers can therefore end up with a legalistic, judgmental, or self-condemning faith, lacking in grace. In suffering, they might say, *"I know I'm a sinner, but I've tried so hard to be good. Why is God punishing me?"* whereas a Love Believer would be more inclined to ask, *"Why would a loving God allow this to happen to me?"*

Righteousness Believers have little difficulty seeing the sin aspect of idolatry, but tend to feel burdened by it as "something else they have to do right." That's not necessarily bad, but it is incomplete. Understanding the impossibility of trying to be good is the first step of fully grasping the significance of the Gospel. The second is rejoicing in the salvation God has provided through Christ.

༄ ༄

When helping someone who is hurting, it is vitally important to listen for true Gospel understanding. Only through the salvation provided in Christ is the joy and freedom of God wholly possible. Years ago, for example, the elderly mother of a pastor asked me for help in considering the physical and emotional trials of her life from a biblical perspective. Thinking

I was just covering the checkmarks, I asked her, "Who is Jesus to you?"

"The Son of God," she replied thoughtfully. Then she added, "I couldn't get through my day without Him. I pray to Him without ceasing."

I had fully expected her to confidently say, "He is my Lord and Savior!" so her answer, while lovely, seemed strangely lacking. Curious and somewhat hesitantly, I asked, "How do you know you're saved?"

"Because I feel close to God," she answered.

We went back and forth like that once or twice more, with me asking pointed Gospel questions, and she just as pointedly avoiding claiming Jesus as her Lord and Savior. I felt awkward asking more—she *was* the mother of a notable Christian pastor, after all. It was possible she was just trying to express that truth in other ways, I thought. We moved on to exploring practical biblical suggestions for her problems.

Years later, I heard she was still struggling; and I realize now that the most important thing I could have done in our time together was discuss the Gospel. How many other people had avoided doing so out of respect for her position, maturity, and enthusiasm for God? She had received a great deal of practical advice from many people; but only the Gospel was going to give her the peace she so desired.

☙ ❧

One afternoon, a young woman named Julie called to complain that her young son threw a tantrum each morning as she tried to get him dressed, causing her to be repeatedly late for work. He never threw a tantrum with his father—only with her—and she was at her wits' end. Nothing she had tried to get her son to cooperate or obey had worked.

There was evidence of idolatry in her frustration and confusion, but she hadn't yet made it clear whether she was asking for help examining her heart or just looking for practical tips on how to get a child ready in the morning. So, I just listened. After a few minutes of sharing her exasperation, she suddenly interrupted herself and asked, "Does God only save believers who are strong enough not to sin?"

I was surprised by the change of topic; but since the question itself revealed a lack of understanding of the grace found in Christ, I asked, "What do you mean by 'believer'?"

"I believe in God," she said, "but I keep getting angry. I've attended so many conferences, read so many books, and been a part of so many Bible studies to learn how to stop being angry, but nothing works! I know I shouldn't get mad so easily, but I keep doing it! What is the matter with me?"

After confirming she wasn't talking about being abusive, I said, "It's good you believe in God, Julie, but lots of people believe in God without being a 'believer.' What I mean is, do you believe in Jesus as your Lord and Savior?"

Sighing, she asked, "So, I'm not a believer?"

"I don't know. Have you 'given yourself up to Him, taken yourself out of your own keeping and entrusted yourself entirely into His keeping'?" (Acts 16:31 AMP).

"I asked Him to come into my life," she said tentatively. "But I still sin."

"You can't *not* sin; at least not in the fullest sense of the word. The more you grow in righteousness, the more sensitive you become to your own capacity to sin. That may sound awful, but it is the very thing which leads you to rejoice in the grace of salvation by faith in Jesus Christ."

I went on to explain how asking Jesus into her life was not necessarily the same as asking Him to be her Lord and Savior, and that being saved did not mean she would never struggle with anger. Together we rejoiced in the way God was using her areas of weakness and temptation to bring her into a deeper understanding of His salvation, truth, and grace.

ꟹ ꟹ

The adoptive mother of a young college student asked if I would meet with her daughter over lunch to chat about some difficult times the daughter was having, discuss her past sin and drug use, and look at upcoming situations that were troubling her. The mother was a friend, so we set a date; and I looked forward to the visit.

When we met, Sydney spoke openly of loving God, referred to herself as a believer, freely confessed sinful decisions, and commented how her faith had grown as a result of several very painful things that had happened to her over the past year. She admitted she was struggling with what she called "a life-time of rejection"—by her birth mother, best friends, co-workers, and most recently, a potential fiancé. Confident and smart, charming and honest, Sydney readily shared her heart and easily identified desires related to those circumstances that could be idols of her heart.

When I asked about her faith, Sydney said she had accepted Christ as a young girl at summer camp, had been homeschooled by her adoptive parents—strong Christians who loved her and whom she loved, and she was now active in college Bible studies. Everything in her words, demeanor, and attitude implied a belief in Jesus as her Lord and Savior.

It might seem unrealistic to expect God to do anything significant in a person's heart in just a couple of hours, but He often does. When a believer realizes they have been worshipping something other than God, the Holy Spirit moves in their heart to conviction. Previous preoccupation with their own pain and others' sin is replaced with godly sorrow, leading to repentance, joy, and peace. It really can happen that fast.

Sydney quickly grasped the concept of idolatry, so I anticipated seeing God move in her heart in some significant way. The barest hint of a tear appeared, but it disappeared just as quickly. Two hours into our conversation, she was as calm and self-assured as when we had first greeted one another.

The visit had gone by fast and I had enjoyed the conversation, but it was a long time for a believer-in-pain to consider God's holiness without any discernable stirring of the Holy Spirit. She was responding the way a non-believer would respond to the truth about wrong worship. I was confused.

At one point, Sydney described how offended she had once been when a good friend had invited her to a revival, saying it might do her some good. I was concerned it would anger her if I asked whether or not she was a believer. Somewhat hesitantly I said, "You've referred to yourself as a believer. I was wondering what you meant by that?"

"Someone who believes in God," she said, casually.

"Well," I said, choosing my words carefully, "a believer *does* believe in God, but who is *Jesus* to you?"

"You know, the same as God," she replied.

I wondered how a believer could seem so disinterested in Christ. Would she have responded so nonchalantly if she were describing a fireman who had rescued her from a burning building, or a lifeguard who had saved her from a shark attack? Where was the depth of gratitude for what Jesus had done?

Perhaps she was just having a crisis of faith, I thought, or struggling with the rejection of God that follows sin. Maybe she had said the prayer of salvation as a good work—rather than out of conviction and the desire to be saved. Her answers sounded more like a non-believer's answers. Had she just adopted the role of a believer to please her family or "accepted Christ" without understanding her need for a Savior?

As I was thinking on these things, Sydney herself wondered aloud whether or not she really was a believer. I didn't rush to say she was or try to "make her saved." I just shared the Gospel in full and prayed with her that God would reveal His Truth to her.

Had I had not been listening for evidence of an understanding of the Gospel, focused on her practical problems or the psychology and grief of rejection, or let fear of offending her keep me from sharing the Gospel, I would have completely missed the most important thing of all.

UPDATE 2018: I unexpectedly reconnected with Sydney recently and learned she has endured some very painful experiences in the years since we first met. We continue to talk from time to time, and each time I remind her of God's truth of the Gospel. I join her parents in praying that one day, she will fully embrace the new life only He can give.

Catherine was a Righteousness Believer raised in a church that taught an understanding of God's wrath against sin, but said little about His mercy or the grace of His love. Both she and her husband had stopped attending church years ago, so it was with some hesitation she attended a four-week seminar on idolatry. With a full understanding of God's righteousness *and* His love, she asked Jesus to be her Lord and Savior that week, and some time later sent me this testimony:

Catherine's Testimony

I don't think there was ever a time in my life that I doubted God's existence, and I have always had some degree of faith. I grew up in the Catholic Church, but for a long time had felt that I was missing something and I longed for the kind of relationship that my Christian friends seemed to have with God. For various reasons I had essentially stopped going to church, but after a difficult few years I was hitting a pretty low point in my life. I kept feeling this tugging on my heart, this need for God in my life.

When you helped me understand how my heart was being idolatrous, I realized that I needed to let go of my need for control (which was controlling me) and put God first. Through aiming to please God, instead of trying to control everything myself, I began to see God at work and experience His love so clearly in my life. I felt like these random puzzle pieces just started falling into place and everything made so much sense.

By then, I realized I needed Jesus. Two days later, I got down on my knees and asked Him to be my Lord and Savior! After that, the Bible really came alive for me, and I started grasping the enormity of who Jesus was and what that decision meant.

What really changed things for me was what you said about how much God loved me, and that my heart's goal should be to please God before anything else. First, I had to get my heart right with God. Learning to submit to what God wanted for me had a profound effect on my life. I found such peace and joy, and have seen God at work in every aspect of my life since then. My relationships with my husband and children have also improved dramatically.

This understanding was really the catalyst in my walk with Jesus, and the last year has been one of incredible spiritual growth, with the fundamentals of pleasing God and examining my heart as the foundation. I have learned when I stop thinking I can control the future—if only I knew how—and trust the future to God, He does remarkable things. I have been totally awestruck by this on numerous occasions, and my faith has become real and strong by seeing every place where God has been—and continues to be—at work in my life.

☙ ❧

13. A Matter of Faith

Miranda's Story

Miranda was a "Love Believer," having grown up in a church where God's love was frequently preached, but little was ever mentioned about sin. She had spent the past year serving as a lay leader in one of the ministries at her local church, while secretly struggling with depression and anger at God. The first thing she said to me when the pastor's wife introduced us was that she didn't care whether she lived or died.

"I am not going to kill myself," she said, "but I lay in bed and wish I didn't have to live. I don't understand why God has allowed me to suffer so much."

She gave me permission to ask Listening Questions, but soon became quite irritated with me. "I don't see how these are relevant!" she declared, crossing her arms in a huff.

When I assured her I was only trying to hear and understand her heart, not judge her, she relaxed. Soon she was even enjoying identifying various areas of idolatry on her own. I noticed, however, her excitement seemed only intellectual, without any obvious spiritual conviction. So, I took a chance and asked who Jesus was to her.

Surprisingly, she replied in an oddly irritated, almost sarcastic, manner. "I know, I know," she said, rolling her eyes, "He's the bridge." Waving a hand, she added, "You know, my Lord and Savior."

She had mentioned accepting Christ as a child, but this strangely annoyed claim of faith was more like a memorized and wearisome school assignment, than a true profession of faith. If she was truly a believer, something was definitely missing in her understanding of the Gospel that she should have such a lack of awe of salvation and be living so far outside the joy of the Lord. The turning point in our conversation came when she said, "I feel like I'm such an awful person."

My natural inclination would have been to assure her she was not awful, and tell her she was a beloved child of God made perfect in His sight. Those things are all true for a believer in Christ, but it was not my prerogative to judge whether she was a believer or not, and I thought it best not to assure her of something I didn't know to be true.

What I *did* tell her was that she had just spoken the second most important thing anyone needed to know. "Yes! You *are* an awful person!" I said with excitement. "You were born a 'dirty, rotten, sinner,' and so was I. There is nothing you can do to be good, which is exactly what God *wants* you to know—and what a wonderful thing it is to know!"

She looked at me, a little shocked.

"What do we get from knowing God's commands?" I continued, with some excitement.

"How to be good?" she replied.

"Paul explains that God's commands were given as a guardian until Christ came, so that we might be saved by faith (Galatians 3:24). They tell us what God requires for righteousness, and in so doing make us aware of sin, our rebellious self-sufficiency and our need for mercy and grace (Romans 3:20; 7:9-10). Until we grasp that, we can never truly understand God's love in providing a Savior."

I stood and began reading aloud in a dramatic voice from Romans 7, pacing and waving my arms about as if frustrated with my own stubborn sinfulness. "I do not understand my own actions. For I do not do what I want, but I do the very thing I hate. Now if I do what I do not want, I agree with the law, that it is good. So, now it is no longer I who do it, but sin that dwells within me. For I know that nothing good dwells in me, that is, in my flesh. For I have the desire to do what is right, but not the ability to carry it out. For I do not do the good I want, but the evil I do not want is what I keep on doing!" (Romans 7:15-19).

Pausing, I turned to her and asked, "Does that sound like you, when you first walked in?

"Yes," she admitted.

I continued as I walked toward her. "Now if I do what I do not want, it is no longer I who do it, but sin that dwells within me (v. 20)." Sitting down, I invited her to read the last two verses aloud, in first person.

"O unhappy and pitiable and wretched woman that I am, who will release and deliver me from this body of death? Thanks be to God Who delivers me through Jesus Christ!" (vv. 24-25).

"Do you see?" I asked, gently.

"Yes," she said with tears in her eyes, "I see." She prayed a prayer of salvation and her face was transformed by God's peace. Eighteen months later she sent me the following written testimony:

Miranda's Testimony

When we first met, I told you I wanted to die. It's not that I wanted to kill myself, I just didn't want to exist anymore: I desperately wanted to go to sleep and not wake up. Events of the last fifteen years—three marriages; two divorces; an abortion; the deaths of my brother, mother and father just a few months apart; becoming a stepmother to two teenagers; and leaving behind friends to move to a new country had caught up with me. I felt utterly defeated and wondered why God would allow me to suffer so much, and I was despairing over my idols (though I didn't know they were idols, yet).

In those years, I had tried so hard to fit in and do what was expected, but I never moved forward. Worse, the things I longed for—family, friends, love, happiness, belonging and financial security—seemed to slip farther away as I compromised myself time and time again.

Last year my husband and I moved and for the first time since leaving school, I did not work. Part of me knew this was a blessing from God, and I felt something important was going to happen that couldn't happen if I was working—but another part of me, the part that finds her value in what she does, felt worthless. Within six months, I had started a course of anti-depressants. These took the edge off, but the real issues were still there.

One morning I met our pastor's wife for coffee. I hadn't told her anything about my past before, but that morning I opened up and told her everything. She said, 'There's someone I'd like you to meet' and a few days later introduced me to you.

I had already seen any number of psychologists, counselors, and therapists. I had tried yoga, meditation, journaling, regression therapy, Cognitive Behavioral Therapy, Emotional Freedom Therapy, bereavement counseling, hypnotherapy, NLP, Guided Therapeutic Imagery, chanting mantras and positive affirmations, reciting Catholic incantations and the Rosary, and receiving prayer at church. So, it's fair to say I was skeptical of what you could offer, but I was also open. I thought if He could love you and use you, then maybe it was possible for me, too.

We spent an amazing and emotional two and a half hours together, during which time I realized I had idols in my heart regarding my desire to be loved, to not be poor again, to have good health, and for my mom's acceptance.

Most importantly, though, was what happened when I acknowledged I was a 'dirty rotten sinner.' I knew I had done bad things and sinned, but I had never recognized my essential state of being as sinful. Now I realize nothing I ever do will be enough to earn my way into heaven—I can only confess my sins and receive the forgiveness made available by Jesus Christ dying on the cross. God loves me. Full stop.

I know now that I do not belong to myself—I belong to God. It is the Lord who has made me, and I am his (Psalm 100:3). Today, I feel like I am seeing in full color for the first time, like the scales have truly fallen from my eyes and I see myself for what I am: a sinner who was brought to repentance and saved by God's grace. Now I live by faith and by the Spirit. The condemnation and self-hatred are gone. I don't wake up each morning wondering why I'm still here . . . but thanking God I am.

☙ ❧

The true stories in this chapter were not intended as self-righteous judgments on other people's faith. They were simply true demonstrations of how carefully listening to someone can reveal unexpected opportunities to share the Gospel.

This is important, because the Gospel is the key to everything. Without Jesus Christ as Lord *and* Savior there is no lasting life transformation, no deliverance from the guilt of sin, no spiritual peace that surpasses all circumstances, no hope of eternal life. Intellectual ability cannot give us these things. Physical or spiritual strength cannot set us free from the debilitating desire to be in control of our own lives. Resisting the call to surrender to God always leads to rebellion, anger, guilt, shame, and death.

So, in every situation of our lives—in every *moment* of our lives—we have a choice: to seek to please ourselves and continue to struggle; or to lay down our self-authority and surrender ourselves to God. There is no middle ground, for He alone gives peace.

☙ ❧☙ ❧

The Gospel, as Taught by Jesus

This is my Father's will and His purpose, that everyone who sees the Son and believes in and cleaves to and trusts in and relies on Him should have eternal life and I will raise him up [from the dead] at the last day. No one is able to come to Me, unless the Father Who sent Him attracts and draws him and gives him the desire to come to Me. All who are drawn and have the desire to come to Me shall be taught of God. Everyone who has listened and learned from the Father comes to me. He who believes in Me has (now possesses) eternal life, and I will raise him up [from the dead] in the last day. (He will) dwell continually in Me and I in him. Just as the living Father sent Me and I live by the Father, even so everyone who believes in me shall live through and because of Me (From John 6:37-57).

A Prayer of Salvation

I confess I am a sinner, Lord. I believe Jesus was sent by You, and was declared to be the Son of God, according to the Spirit of holiness, by His resurrection from the dead.[32] I confess my sins, and ask Jesus Christ to be my Lord and Savior, "Who, through the eternal Spirit, offered Himself without blemish to God" and whose blood purifies my conscience from dead works to serve the living God.[33] Continue to work in me, oh God, in order that I might be made more like Him and submit myself to You in increasing measure. In the name of Jesus Christ, amen.

Those who pay regard to vain idols forsake their hope of steadfast love (Jonah 2:8).

Appendix a: References

Appendix 6: Examples

Examples, con't.

Use of These Materials

Individual quotations of up to 200 words of the author's words from this work may be used for ministry purposes without written permission, provided proper attribution is given as follows: "Excerpt from *Discerning Idols: Having a God Empowered® Heart,* by K. B. Haught." None of the stories, emails or conversations may be used without express written permission.

Quotations of more than 200 words, or of a specific story, example, or testimony, require written permission before use. Please email info@godempowered.com with contextual references and purpose, in order to request permission.

About Karen Haught

Karen Haught spent thirty years in the corporate world, first as an entrepreneur and then as an executive in both public and private companies, before becoming a certified biblical counselor in 2007—something she credits with changing her life.

Her first book, "The God Empowered® Wife: How Strong Women Can Help Their Husbands Become Godly Leaders," (2008) is the story of how God transformed her heart and her marriage. That book has been translated into four languages and helped restore marriages around the world. "Discerning Idols" was initially a chapter in that book, but is now an even larger book in its own right.

As a speaker, Karen is well-known for incorporating lively demonstrations, true stories, and case studies into her workshops and conferences—which she has shared with audiences across the USA as well as Asia-Pacific, Europe, Australia, and Africa. Karen and her husband currently reside in Houston, Texas, where they are active in their local church.

kbhaught@godempowered.com
www.godempowered.com

Scripture Index

Endnotes

[1] The basics of the "Y" chart are credited to Dr. Mark Dutton D.Min,

[2] This concept of "Everything everyone does is really for selfish reasons," became popular with the public due to Ayn Rand's material in the mid 1950's; however it initiated from philosophical discussions in the late 18th century, and earlier.

[3] The phrase, "Big, hairy, audacious, goal [BHAG]" was coined by Jim Collins and Jerry I. Porras, in their book, Built to Last; Harper Business, 1994.

[4] I have chosen not to provide the name of the pastor and church responsible for this sermon, because my purpose is for the reader to learn to discern biblical accuracy, no matter the source—rather than draw attention to a particular ministry.

5 This popular quote has been attributed variously to Richard Bach, Joseph Adam Jonas, Douglas Horton, Sting, Peter Max, Chantal Sicile, and others; but the earliest print version of this particular wording is in a book by teacher Jess Lair, referencing a student who submitted it on an index card as part of an assignment (www.quoteinvestigator.com). However, it is identical in principle to the countercultural philosophies of the 1950's and 1960's espoused by Alan Watts and his predecessor, Aldous Huxley; as well as the philosophies of Buddhism.

[6] A Gomesi is a traditional Ugandan dress with large puffy sleeves.

[7] You can see a video demonstration of this, with women in Zambia acting it out in their native language, under the "International" menu option on my website at www.godempowered.com.

[8] Alan Watts (1915-1973) is credited with these specific phrases and the example of floating or sinking. However, similar philosophies and human observations or "discoveries" of what are essentially God's laws can be found in both religious and non-religious teachings throughout all of human history.

[9] Teachings on a "God-shaped hole in our hearts can be traced back to Blaise Pascal, who wrote: "What else does this craving, and this helplessness, proclaim but that there was once in man a true happiness, of which all that now remains is the empty print and trace? This he tries in vain to fill with everything around him, seeking in things that are not there the help he cannot find in those that are, though none can help, since this infinite abyss can be filled only with an infinite

and immutable object; in other words by God himself." Blaise Pascal, Pensées VII(425) 1662.

[10] James 3:10 (AMP).

[11] The image of these symptoms as "caution flags" is credited to Amy Baker, Director of Ministry Resources, Faith Resources; Counselor & Instructor, Faith Biblical Counseling Ministries; Director of Ministry Resources, Faith Church; Director of Counseling, Vision of Hope. Lafayette, Indiana.

[12] Some of the questions for the Idols Test were taken or adapted from Ken Sande, The Peacemaker: A Biblical Guide to Resolving Personal Conflict, Baker Books, Grand Rapids, MI 2005. p 115-116. Used with permission. Others were compiled or adapted from the teachings of Randy Patten and various Fellows of the Association of Certified Biblical Counselors.)

[13]Thanks to Randy Patten and others with the Association of Certified Biblical Counselors (www.biblicalcounseling.com) (formerly National Association of Nouthetic Counselors) for this question, and various alternatives to the others.

[14] Wurmbrand, Richard. Tortured for Christ. Living Sacrifice Book Company, Bartlesville, OK, 1998

[15]http://www.desiringgod.org/resource-library/taste-see-articles/dont-waste-your-cancer, from Piper, John. "Don't Waste Your Cancer," pamphlet, Crossway Books, Wheaton, IL, 2010, 2011.

[16] An example of a two page handout explaining the four rules of communication as outlined in Ephesians can be found at https://ibcd.org/wp-content/uploads/2012/10/Four-Rules-of-Communication.pdf

[17] Prager, Dennis. "Judaism's Sexual Revolution: Why Judaism Rejected Homosexuality." http://catholiceducation.org/articles/homosexuality/ho0003.html.

[18] Matthew 23:26

[19] See my book, The God Empowered Wife, for more practical information on how modern wives can honor God in their marriages.

[20] Isaiah 53:3

[21] Mark 10:18; Romans 3:23; 1 John 1:8-10

[22] Proverbs 28:26; Jeremiah. 17:9; Matthew 15:19

[23] John 14:6

[24] Romans 7, 8; Galatians 5, 6; Ephesians 2:8, 1 Thessalonians 4

[25] Galatians 2:20; 5:24; Matthew 10:38; 16:24; John 12:24,25; Romans 12:21; Galatians 5

[26] Matthew 6:33; Philippians 4:19.

[27] Leviticus 11:44; Proverbs 3:5; 2 Timothy 3:16; Psalm 19:7; 1 Peter 1:16; 2 Peter 1:20.

[28] Isaiah 46:10; Psalm 47:2; 1 Timothy 1:17

[29] An artifact in Greek mythology. The "box" was actually a large jar given to Pandora which contained all the evils of the world. Pandora opened the jar and all the evils flew out, leaving only "Hope" inside once she had closed it again. Today the phrase "to open Pandora's box" means to perform an action that may seem small or innocent, but that turns out to have severely detrimental and far-reaching negative consequences. See https://en.wikipedia.org/wiki/Pandora%27s_box.

[30] Haught, K. B., The God Empowered Wife. Intendion. 2008.

[31] The story of Abigail and Nabal can be found in 1 Samuel 25

[32] Romans 1:4

[33] Hebrews 9:14

The following pages have been left blank for your notes.

53994677R00177

Made in the
USA
Lexington, KY